ntremont

Pompeii

Troy
Pergamon
Çatalhöyük
Akrotiri
Ephesus
Knossos
Palmyra
Tanis
Babylon
Leptis
Magnis
Alexandria
Petra
Persepolis
Harappa
Mohenjo-
Daro

Fujiwara

Meroe

Angkor

Great
Zimbabwe

LOST CITIES

OF THE ANCIENT WORLD

LOST CITIES
OF THE ANCIENT WORLD

JOEL LEVY

NEW HOLLAND

First published in 2008 by New Holland Publishers (UK) Ltd
London • Cape Town • Sydney • Auckland
www.newhollandpublishers.com

10 9 8 7 6 5 4 3 2 1

Garfield House, 86–88 Edgware Road, London W2 2EA, UK
80 McKenzie Street, Cape Town 8001, South Africa
Unit 1, 66 Gibbes Street, Chatswood, NSW 2067, Australia
218 Lake Road, Northcote, Auckland, New Zealand

ISBN: 978 184537 942 1

Editorial Direction: Jo Hemmings and Rosemary Wilkinson
Senior Editor: Kate Parker
Editorial Assistant: Nicole Whitton
Design and cover design: Alan Marshall at Heron Recreations
Production: Melanie Dowland

Reproduction by Pica Digital PTE Ltd, Singapore
Printed and bound by Tien Wah Press, Singapore

Front cover: El Castillo at Chichen Itza; Back cover (left to
right): frieze of Isis and Io at Pompeii, the Treasury at Petra,
detail from Babylon's Ishtar Gate; Page 1: Petra, view of the
Treasury from the Siq; Page 2: The Acropolis at Pergamum;
Page 3: detail from the Ishtar Gate, Babylon; Opposite:
Bayon face towers, Angkor Thom; Page 6 main image: Arch
of Severus, Leptis Magna; Page 7: Temple and statue of
Apollo, Pompeii.

CONTENTS

Introduction 8

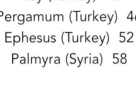

INTRODUCTION

From the Neolithic to the Middle Ages, from the deserts of Arizona to the plains of Japan – this book tells the stories of lost cities from many different times and places. However, for many of the 'lost cities' described, one or both of the terms could be considered contentious. What constitutes a city, rather than a town or simply a settlement? What does it mean to be 'lost'? For the purposes of covering a wide, varied and interesting range of subjects, both of these terms have been interpreted loosely.

City-living

What constitutes a city? In a classical, conventional sense, a city was a large urban settlement with certain characteristics. While there was not necessarily a minimum population threshold, a city was usually distinguished by an organized, stratified population, with an elite and possibly a ruler. Below them was a class of people who did not practise agriculture, or at least did not rely on it for their livelihood, earning their money through crafts or trading. And below these, the large mass of common people who supported the other groups through their agriculture. This level of social 'development' (inverted commas are appropriate because such a development rarely benefits the lower orders, as shown by analysis of skeletal remains over time, which tend to show shorter life expectancy, poorer diet, more disease and, in general, lower quality of life before and after the transition to a stratified, hierarchical society) was only usually possible once agricultural technology had advanced sufficiently to allow farmers to move beyond subsistence production and to produce surpluses.

Associated with this social organization are other characteristics that usually defined a city. Some level of geographical differentiation was usually involved – in other words, in a city, different areas serve different functions. The centre might have been where the ruling elite lived, and/or where administrative or military functions were based, while other neighbourhoods might have been specialized by class or employment (e.g. there might have been an artisans' quarter). Commonly there was a religious precinct or neighbourhood. Associated with some of these functions was the presence of public architecture – buildings that did not serve an exclusively private function, such as squares, forums, temples, banquet halls, etc. Many of these features were considered to be among the defining characteristics of civilization and so the development of cities also becomes part of the definition of civilization.

Most of the settlements covered in this book meet these criteria for 'cityhood', but not all of them. The first place described in the book is Çatalhöyük, a Neolithic settlement in Turkey that fails to meet most of the criteria, while other entries such as Entremont, an ancient Gaulish *oppidum* (Iron Age fortified settlement) in southern France; Akrotiri, a port on what was the Aegean island of Thera and Machu Picchu, the mountain-top citadel of the Incas, meet some of the criteria but were probably too small to realistically be described as more than towns. These are included partly because of their

El Caracol or 'The Snail': a building at the Maya city of Chichen Itza, which functioned as an observatory. It is named for the spiral staircase within.

fascinating individual stories and partly because they mark important milestones in urban history.

Other places in the book, such as Great Zimbabwe, Knossos and the Chaco Canyon pueblos, challenge some of these notions of cityhood. At these three locations the primary vestiges of the settlement consist of a single central structure, which, although very large, may not even have been primarily residential. Yet they almost certainly constituted the central focus of their respective cultures and societies, and were probably surrounded by zones of habitation that for whatever reason have not left a mark. Even settlements as big as the enormous temple complex at Angkor, the monolithic ruins of Tiwanaku in Bolivia and the mighty remnants of Tikal in Guatemala have been characterized at times as largely uninhabited ceremonial structures rather than 'real' cities (although in all three cases this theory has been largely disproved). So it makes sense to adopt a fluid definition of what constitutes a city.

Lost and Found

There is also room for debate over what constitutes being 'lost'. The archetypal lost cities are probably the great Mayan ruins such as Tikal. In its day Tikal was a huge metropolis of up to 60,000 people, covering 121.75 square kilometres (47 square miles), yet 500 years after its fall it had become 'invisible' enough for a Spanish army to pass within a few miles yet have no conception of its existence. It was to maintain this low profile for a further three and a half centuries. A once thriving metropolis that had ruled a vast swathe of Central America had fallen off the map, its existence utterly forgotten by all but a handful of local people.

This was only possible because of a unique combination of circumstances: an ecosystem with the potential to support a dense population for long enough for a mighty city to flourish, yet harsh enough to consume an entire civilization within a century (see page 173). Together with

the comparative poverty of the region in terms of natural resources (at least as far as European invaders were concerned) and the wholesale obliteration of Mayan culture by the Spanish, this strangely double-edged environment meant that entire cities could be abandoned in their prime and quickly obscured beneath a thick veneer of jungle.

In most of the rest of the world circumstances are very different, and for many of the other cities covered in this book, the term 'lost' must be loosely defined. It can apply to cities that remained well known until modern times, such as Babylon (the approximate location of which was never really lost) and even to ones that remained continuously inhabited, such as Alexandria or Tenochtitlán, although in both of these cases the present city is very different from that which previously occupied the site, justifying their inclusion. In general, lost cities in the Old World left visible remains, such as mounds or ruins, and were often located in the midst of populous, well-travelled regions. The ancient Indus cities of Harappa and Mohenjo-daro, for instance, were well known to the people of the region through huge mounds from which piles of bricks protruded, even if they were not properly understood. Even the location of ancient Pompeii, buried beneath a thick coating of ash, pumice and the soil of millennia, was known thanks to ancient writings and local folk knowledge.

Urban Apocalypse

How do cities become lost? There are really two parts to this question: firstly, why did people stop living in the city? And secondly, how was the physical fabric of the city lost or obscured so that it passed out of knowledge? Perhaps the most straightforward answer to both of these is a sudden disaster – natural or manmade – of some sort. Pompeii and Akrotiri were both thriving cities until volcanoes erupted nearby. Troy – or at least one phase of its occupation – may have been razed by a horde of Greek invaders. Entremont was besieged and taken by Roman legions, who carried off into slavery most of the residents, returning a few decades later to polish off the remnants. Tenochtitlán was simply replaced by the conquistadors, who constructed a new city in its place.

Beyond this, however, it is possible to identify several factors that can contribute to the decline of a city:

Geographical: Cities are founded at particular spots because those places have environmental, strategic or economic advantages, or possibly because they have religious/spiritual significance (although this is hard to reconstruct without good contemporary sources). If something happens to remove those advantages, the city may lose its raison d'être, and this can be a relatively straightforward reason for urban decline. For instance, a city built on a river that changes course or dries up is obviously at risk of losing its economic and environmental underpinnings. Examples of this include Tanis, an ancient Egyptian city built on a branch of the Nile that silted up and Mohenjo-daro, which suffered when one nearby river changed course and another dried up altogether. Similarly Ephesus was originally a thriving port city, but is now several miles inland. Even in these cases, however, such straightforward physical factors are only part of the story.

Economic: Trade routes, like rivers, can change course, and this may affect cities with economic rationales. A good example is Petra, a site originally settled because it combined defensibility with water sources (and possibly for religious reasons), but that flourished because important trade routes passed nearby. When the Romans built a new road that bypassed the city and redirected the bulk of trade, Petra lost its economic basis and slipped into decline. Broader economic factors may also play a part. The decline of Leptis Magna, a Roman port city in North Africa, began with an empire-wide economic crisis in the 3rd century CE.

Environmental: Archaeologists and historians are increasingly coming to understand the importance of environmental factors in the decline of cities. Cities, with their large, high-density populations and hunger for resources – from food and water to firewood, construction materials and raw material for industry – place a heavy load on the environment. Cultures that have lived in a sustainable fashion for millennia can quickly find that their relationship with the environment has changed when they make the shift to urban living. And because environmental collapse can be a very rapid, sudden phenomenon that occurs when certain tipping points are reached, calamity can come upon a city in a very short time, and often just at the exact point when it seems to reach its zenith. The purest examples of this phenomenon are in the Americas, where urban centres such as the Chaco Canyon pueblos and the Classic Mayan cities disturbed relatively fragile ecosystems, tipping them into meltdown with catastrophic consequences for the inhabitants. In the southern lowlands of the Mayan region it is thought that over a million people probably died and/or emigrated, after 600 years of increasingly magnificent urban achievement collapsed in little over a century. Similar processes may have contributed to the abandonment of cities such as Angkor, Great Zimbabwe and Cahokia. In most cases, natural climate change may also have been involved, with dry periods and droughts exacerbating or triggering environmental collapse.

Political: For much of human history, empires and kingdoms have been ruled by despots and dictators with absolute power. Such individuals are able to found cities by personal decree (albeit for strategic or economic reasons), such as Alexander the Great and Alexandria, Darius the Great and Persepolis and Tenmu and Fujiwara-kyo, but this also means that they can end them in similar fashion. For instance, when later emperors decided to found a new capital to the north, Fujiwara-kyo was stripped of all useful material and abandoned. Generally, however, political factors work over a longer period and in conjunction with other factors. Alexandria, for instance, suffered a long decline after the Islamic conquest when its new rulers founded a new capital at Cairo. Several other cities, including Tanis, Meroe and Angkor, lost status, power, money and eventually residents to competing cities or when political developments sidelined them.

War: Many of the cities described in this book, though not destroyed in a single battle, were tipped into decline by acts of violence. Examples include: Persepolis, according to legend set alight by a vengeful Alexander; Leptis Magna, which never fully recovered from its conquest by Vandals and from an even worse raid by Berbers and Palmyra, taken by the Romans at the height of its glory.

Exhaustion: Sometimes a city can simply become exhausted by a combination of insults and injuries. Babylon, for instance, was among the largest cities in the world for millennia and bounced back from devastating episodes several times in its history, maintaining its pre-eminence through a succession of empires. Finally, however, constant warfare following the collapse of Alexander's short-lived empire drained its human and material resources to the point of no return. Eventually even the irrigation network that enabled the region to support such a large city fell into disrepair. A similar tale of woe bled the life out of Ephesus, once the greatest city in Asia Minor (modern-day Turkey). Between the 7th and 15th centuries CE it was repeatedly assaulted, sacked and otherwise abused, as well as suffering from malaria, coastal retreat and economic breakdown.

Dead and Buried

The well-preserved remains of the Chaco Canyon pueblos show that, when conditions are right, the physical fabric of a lost city can survive remarkably well. So why have so many cities been physically lost? How can a metropolis of massive buildings physically disappear from view?

The primary factor is the simple passage of time. It is easy to underestimate the speed and power of natural forces, and the need to constantly maintain and repair the physical fabric of a city if it is not to fall quickly into ruin. In tropical conditions, a few years of neglect can result in a covering of dense vegetation, and tree roots can pry apart even the best masonry, tumbling huge blocks. The impressive structures of Chichen Itza and Angkor, for instance, are largely the result of intensive reconstruction and salvage programmes – when rediscovered some of them were little more than piles of shattered masonry. In dryer conditions it will take much longer for structures to be lost, but the combination of natural erosion, which wears down structures, and natural and anthropogenic deposition, which covers them up, can turn even a great city into an amorphous mound (also known as a 'tell') that resembles a natural hill. Many cities continue to be partly inhabited during their long decline, when there is unlikely to be much of a municipal waste disposal service, so rubbish and dirt will quickly build up. The mound of Hissarlik (also known as Troy) in the Dardanelles, for instance, proved to contain at least nine phases of occupation, despite having been uninhabited for at least 1,300 years.

More dramatic natural forces can speed the process. Many ancient Roman and Greek cities were built in zones of high seismic activity and thus were vulnerable to earthquakes and occasionally volcanoes and tsunami. Alexandria, for instance, was badly damaged by numerous earthquakes and also suffered from a more gradual consequence of plate tectonics, which was a subsidence of the North African coast and a rise in sea level. As a result, much of the core of ancient Alexandria is currently underwater.

Nature often takes a back seat to human activity. When a city was conquered it was often sacked: walls were overthrown, buildings smashed up and looted and finally the whole was put to the torch. Archaeologists sometimes discover the tell-tale layer of carbon that marks the fiery end of a city or at least of one phase of its occupation, as at Troy VIIa, considered by many to be the Troy of the *Iliad*. Tenochtitlán was levelled house by house in a long and bitter siege by the Spanish and their native allies.

Among the most destructive forces to operate on lost cities are the local people, often living in much reduced circumstances to those that fuelled the growth and maintenance of the original metropolis, and for whom the remains on their doorstep constitute resources rather than heritage. Specifically, an ancient city was often a rich source of worked, dressed blocks of high-quality stone, which could otherwise be obtained only at great expense and effort, and of millions of bricks. The remains of Harappa in the Indus Valley, for instance, were devastated in the 19th century when plundered by workers quarrying bricks as ballast for the nearby railway. Most of the fabric of Tanis in Egypt was lost to lime burners, who used its great limestone blocks as raw material. By contrast, the ruins of Leptis Magna have survived in an excellent state of preservation because no other cities developed in the area for hundreds of years.

A final point to remember is that, while great public structures like Monks Mound at Cahokia or the amphitheatre at Pergamon were built to last, most of an ancient city was not built for permanence. At sites like Cahokia or Great Zimbabwe the vast majority of buildings were built of perishable natural materials. In most ancient cities even structures of brick and stone were expected to last for little more than a generation, despite constant repair and maintenance. The conservators of Pompeii, for instance, point out that many of the buildings, first excavated in the 18th century, have now been exposed to the elements for more than 200 years, but were originally only intended to stand for a few decades.

Cities in Peril

Many of these factors are still at work today, while new ones increase the risk that the remnants of ancient cities will be irretrievably damaged. Excavation means exposure to the elements and without proper conservation this can spell ruin for ruins, but many of the sites are in poor countries that cannot afford to pay for conservation. In some areas climate change threatens to exacerbate erosion problems. Quarrying of ruins for bricks and blocks continues at many sites and looting is a growing problem as increasing global affluence increases the market for illegal antiquities. Even today, at supposedly protected sites such as Angkor, gangs of art thieves loot whole façades to order. In a final irony, war once again threatens to raze some ancient cities. The physical fabric of Babylon survived millennia of warfare, yet in recent years massive damage has been inflicted by American troops based on and around the ancient site.

Many of the cities in this book are at risk of being lost all over again, this time forever.

Note on Dates Given

Each entry is introduced with a basic fact box, which gives location, key features and dates of construction and abandonment. It is important to note that these dates generally refer to the earliest significant phase of occupation/construction, and the latest date of significant occupation, respectively. Many sites, however, can trace some form of occupation back to long before the first main phase – sometimes to the Stone Age – and in most cases sites were only very gradually completely abandoned, if at all. In many cases a village or semi-permanent nomadic occupation continued at the site into modern times.

THE NEAR AND MIDDLE EAST

Cities first appeared in this part of the world in the Neolithic Era, as early as the 8th millennium BCE, heralding the start of civilization in the conventional sense. It is here, in the Near and Middle East, that humans first settled after migrating out of Africa, and here that a special convergence of circumstances – including plants and animals that could be domesticated, suitable habitats and changes in the climate – led hunter-gatherers to become full-time farmers, and later for the farmers to group together in large settlements. And it was here that the first urban settlements, such as Çatalhöyük, evolved into the first cities, such as Babylon.

The Near and Middle East were also the theatre for some of the greatest dramas of ancient history, from the superpowers of the Bronze Age to the clashing titans of the Classical Era. This chapter includes some of the most evocative places in history, such as the near-mythical Babylon and the legendary Troy, which tell of great wars and the clash of empires. It also includes some of the most beautiful of ancient cities, such as the rock-hewn delights of Petra and the graceful columns of Palmyra.

This region has an unequalled variety and wealth of history and the cities covered reflect this, spanning a stretch of time from the Neolithic Era to Late Antiquity, taking in empires and civilizations from ancient Assyria to the Achaemenids to the Greeks and Romans. Some of the cities, such as Petra and Palmyra, reflect the status of this region as the crossroads of history, their architecture combining elements from Mediterranean and Middle Eastern cultures. Others define the styles of their respective cultures, whether at Babylon, where many of the idioms of the city were invented or at Pergamum, where the Classical city attained perhaps its fullest ideal.

The Monastery at Petra, a rock-cut tomb that probably dates back to the 1st century CE, but which may have been used as a church by Byzantine monks, hence the name. Visible in the centre of the pediment is a giant urn, a characteristic feature of Nabatean architecture.

ÇATALHÖYÜK

LOCATION: CENTRAL TURKEY
DATE OF CONSTRUCTION: *c* 7400 BCE
ABANDONED: *c* 6000 BCE
BUILT BY: NEOLITHIC HUNTER-GATHERER FARMERS
KEY FEATURES: NO STREETS – CONTIGUOUS BUILDINGS WITH ROOF ACCESS; SUB-FLOOR BURIALS; INTERIOR DECORATION, MURALS AND FIGURINES

Described by its original excavator as the earliest city in the world, Çatalhöyük is a Neolithic settlement of almost unprecedented size, with many remarkable features – from its close-packed layout to the wealth of art and symbolism that adorns its walls.

In the Konya Basin area of Anatolia, in central Turkey, two mounds rise above the semi-arid plain, separated by the course of the now extinct Carsamba River. This is the site of Çatalhöyük, Turkish for 'fork-mound', named for a path that forked when it reached the base of the larger mound, Çatalhöyük East. In the Neolithic Era, from 7400–6000 BCE, this was a settlement of up to 8,000 people living in 2,000 houses, covering over 12.25 hectares (30 acres). Although not the first Neolithic settlement – settlements at sites such as Jericho date back to 9000 BCE – it was one of the largest and, significantly, was outside the Levantine area previously thought to be the core of advanced Neolithic civilization. It also proved to be one of the most remarkable prehistoric settlements, thanks to the unusual features uncovered by the two principal digs to explore the site – the excavations of James Mellaart in the late 1950s and early 60s, and the ongoing excavations under Ian Hodder since the 1990s. According to leading archaeologist Colin Renfrew, 'Çatalhöyük is *the* dig of the new millennium.'

The Town With No Streets

The most striking feature of Çatalhöyük was that it had no streets. The houses were packed so close together that they effectively formed a single solid mass and access to each house and travel around the town was via the rooftops. The buildings themselves were rectangular, 11–48 square metres (118–517 square feet) in area and probably one-storey high. They were constructed from mud bricks with wooden posts as roof supports, with flat roofs of wooden beams on top of which bundles of reed were laid and mud was packed on top. Everything was covered with a lime-rich plaster, including internal features of the houses such as ovens, platforms and shelves. A small square opening in the south side of the roof led into the house via a wooden stairway of squared timber. This gave access to the main room, where most of the domestic activity took place. Smaller rooms, thought to be often low-ceilinged and very narrow, led off the main room and were accessed by low doorways; they were probably used for storage. There were no windows or side-doors.

The oven or hearth was situated beneath the ceiling opening to allow smoke to escape. Ash and debris scraped out of the oven made the floor area in this part of the room relatively dirty. It was separated from

cleaner zones of the room by ridges in the floor or by raised platforms, which might be used for sleeping or other purposes. Some were covered with reed mats. In fine weather most activity probably took place on the town's roofs, but during the bitterly cold winters families would have huddled in their snug houses. Experiments with a modern replica of a Çatalhöyük dwelling show that, while in fine weather sunlight through the roof opening would make the interiors, with their white plaster coatings, nice and bright, the ovens/hearths ventilated only poorly and during the night and in the winter the houses must have been very gloomy and filled with smoke. This is confirmed by the finding that

An excavated hearth. The lime-rich mud floors could be shaped with ridges and platforms to divide them up into different functional zones.

Overleaf: Panorama showing the current excavations under Ian Hodder. These have identified at least 80 different buildings, although only a fraction of the site has been excavated.

the bodies of Çatalhöyük residents show deposits of soot along their ribs. This is soot that had accumulated in their lungs from lifetimes of exposure to smoke-filled interiors and that settled onto the ribs as the lung tissue decomposed after death.

The Ancestors Below

Another striking feature of Çatalhöyük was that its inhabitants buried their dead directly beneath their living room floors. The area around the hearth was used for burying babies – probably ones that died in childbirth – and also for storing caches of obsidian (see below), with hollow spaces for pots or other small items. Beneath the raised platforms, however, the bodies of older children and adults were buried, usually wrapped in reed mats or placed in baskets. Some of the skeletons have been found disarticulated, leading to speculation that they may have originally been buried elsewhere or left out to be scavenged and decompose before burial, but current thinking is that in fact these burials have been disturbed by later ones. Sometimes the deceased person's head is missing – these people were probably important or especially revered ancestors, whose skulls might be remodelled with plaster and painted, and kept in the room or buried with someone else.

After a certain period of time – perhaps if a house became decrepit or enough people had been buried in it – the inhabitants would rebuild over the original on the same floorplan. The existing building would be cut down to a height of around 1 metre (3¼ feet) and then carefully filled in. Ritual or talismanic objects were sometimes deliberately placed among the filling material. Then the new house would be raised on top of this foundation. In this way the inhabitants of Çatalhöyük could live in close connection with their ancestors going back centuries, with the rising settlement mound – that reached up to 20 metres (65½ feet) above the surrounding plain with 18 levels of habitation – representing the physical embodiment of their group identity and socio-cultural values.

Leopards and Bulls

The third remarkable feature of Çatalhöyük is the extensive art and symbolism found in the form of its murals and figurines. The prehistoric residents covered their white plaster interiors with a variety of murals, including abstract patterns, such as circles, and colourful and exciting hunting scenes. These include many scenes of men (their gender indicated by their ithyphallic appearance (shown with erect penises) and occasionally by a beard) hunting or sporting with wild animals such as aurochs (giant prehistoric bulls) and leopards. By contrast there are no depictions of farming. Perhaps the most famous mural dates from c 6500 BCE and appears to show a view of the town with the nearby twin-peaked volcano of Hasan Daği in the background; if the interpretation is correct, the mural is the oldest map and/or landscape painting ever discovered.

Other interior decoration included horns of animals mounted on the walls and skulls of animals (and possibly ancestors), remodelled with clay and painted. Other figurines have been recovered from beneath floors and in filled-in rooms. They come in a variety of forms, including animals, non-gender specific humans and, in the upper, later levels of occupation, voluptuous women. A famous example, found in a grain bin where it may have been placed to enhance or ensure fertility, is of a voluptuous woman seated on a chair or throne, flanked by a pair of leopards.

The discovery of examples such as the 'leopard queen' prompted Mellaart to assume they were mother goddess figures, suggesting that the people of Çatalhöyük worshipped a dominant female deity and that they were a matriarchal, female-dominated society. Hodder's research has found little evidence for this, showing rather that there was a lot of equality in gender roles, with men and women equally likely to be represented in high-status burials, eating the same diets and sharing most roles around the house. The one exception is that hunting was probably a male activity and was celebrated in the art of Çatalhöyük while agriculture – probably a female-dominated occupation – was not.

Life in Çatalhöyük

The people of Çatalhöyük had Stone Age technology. They used obsidian (volcanic glass) to make a variety of sharp and functional tools, and also used pottery, weaving and other skills. They had basic agriculture, which became more important to them over the lifetime of the town, and supplemented their diet with hunting and the gathering of wild foods. The area around Çatalhöyük was marshy, providing good water resources and fish and game, as well as the mud and reeds they used for construction.

Each building probably housed a family of between five and ten people, and in fine weather most of their activities would have taken place on the town roofs. Men and women probably shared tasks such as pottery and obsidian tool making, which together with agriculture were the main industries of the town, giving them products they could trade for timber from the nearby hills, for the raw obsidian from Cappadocia about 145 kilometres (90 miles) away, and even for goods from much further afield, such as baskets from Mesopotamia and shells from the Red Sea. Rubbish from each household, including faecal matter, was simply dumped into the spaces around and between buildings, so that they became effectively embedded in a giant midden pile. Ash from the fires and ovens helped to sterilize this waste, but even so there must have been considerable stench and vermin issues.

Today the mound of Çatalhöyük shows two peaks, suggesting that in prehistoric times the town actually consisted of two slightly separate built-up areas. This is consistent with an endogamous culture – one where people marry only within the group, tribe or in this case, settlement. Many such societies are actually split into two sub-groups or tribes, which intermarry (to prevent incestuous marriage), and this may be what is indicated by the twin peaks of the mound. The lack of evidence of any contemporary settlements in the area further suggests that kinship and marriage were heavily localized.

A clay stamp seal in the shape of a bear. Similar wall reliefs had been found, but always with their heads and lower limbs missing, so they were incorrectly identified as goddess figures. Such artefacts may have been used to make impressions on skins and/or bodies.

Ian Hodder questions whether Çatalhöyük can be seen as a city in the proper sense of the word, because its layout and the uniformity of the buildings indicate that there were few or no public spaces or buildings, no central focus, such as a palace or temple, and no evidence of a social hierarchy or specialization of employment. It seems that each household was responsible for and to itself and there is no sign that they formed a township for defensive reasons. The exact reason why they did gather at Çatalhöyük remains a mystery, as do the causes of the town's abandonment in around 6000 BCE. A smaller settlement to the west of the main site was briefly occupied from about 6000–5700 BCE. Did the inhabitants of Çatalhöyük proper simply move, and if so, why?

PERSEPOLIS

LOCATION: FARS PROVINCE, IRAN

DATE OF CONSTRUCTION: 513 BCE

ABANDONED: c 8TH CENTURY CE

BUILT BY: DARIUS THE GREAT OF THE ACHAEMENID PERSIAN EMPIRE

KEY FEATURES: MONUMENTAL TERRACE; GATE OF ALL NATIONS; APADANA AUDIENCE HALL; HALL OF ONE HUNDRED COLUMNS; TOMBS OF THE KINGS; PALACES OF DARIUS AND XERXES; TREASURY AND HAREM; RELIEFS; CLAY TABLETS

In the rocky uplands of modern-day Iran, silent ruins atop a huge terrace bear mute witness to the glory of a long-vanished kingdom – the Achaemenid Empire, sometimes described as the first world empire. Where once a forest of mighty columns supported massive roofs of cedar and teak, today only a few remain. Yet extensive surviving reliefs and carvings attest to the pomp and ceremony that was the lifeblood of this courtly capital.

The ruins of Persepolis lie around 70 kilometres (43½ miles) to the northeast of the city of Shiraz, on the eastern edge of a plain known as the Marv Dasht, in the province of Fars. The name itself is actually a Greek rendition of the original name Parsa, both meaning simply 'city of the Persians'. It was constructed to serve as the ceremonial capital of the Achaemenid Empire.

The Achaemenids were a dynasty of Persian kings who emerged from relative obscurity in the middle of the 6th century BCE when Cyrus II (also known as Cyrus the Great, reign 559–530 BCE) unified the competing kingdoms of Persia and swept across the Middle and Near East to acquire a vast empire, snatching the imperial mantle from its ancient Mesopotamian heartland and conquering territories from the Levant to Bactria and Sogdiana in Central Asia. His heirs extended the empire to Egypt, Asia Minor and into Greece, creating a globe-spanning polity that was the first to connect the Mediterranean world to the borders of India and China in a single kingdom.

New Emperor, New Capital

Cyrus made his capital at Pasargadae, but after the death of his successor Cambyses (522 BCE) there was an intense struggle for the throne that ended when Darius I (again later known as 'the Great', reign 521–486 BCE) assumed the crown. To bolster the legitimacy of his claim and assert majesty and dominion in his own right he founded a new and glorious capital, a city of such splendour that it would proclaim and affirm his right to rule the world as the king of kings. Accordingly work was begun on a site chosen for its impressive aspect, where a vast and imposing terrace of stone would support great buildings calculated to awe subjects and visiting rulers alike. The discovery by archaeologists of construction sites where the builders' rubble had yet to be removed shows that work continued on the site under Darius's successors, right up until the Achaemenid Empire was conquered in the late 4th century BCE.

The Terrace and Main Buildings

A huge terrace of stone was partly carved out of the rocky hill (known as the Kuh-e Rahmat or 'Mountain of

Mercy') that the site backs on to, and raised up above the surrounding plain. The terrace was 450 metres (1,476 feet) long and 300 metres (984 feet) wide – covering over 125,000 square metres (over 1⅓ million square feet), and rose 14 metres (46 feet) above the plain. Although there is no trace of them now, ancient sources record that the terrace was bounded by three huge walls, the greatest of which was said to be 27 metres (88½ feet) high. Massive staircases from the plain led up to the terrace, with steps wide and low enough for horses to pass freely up and down.

The main staircase onto the site was on the northwest corner, leading to a huge gatehouse built by Xerxes – known as either Xerxes' Gate or the Gate of All Nations (symbolizing the extent of Achaemenid rule), the ruins of which still remain. Massive double doors of wood bound in metal gave on to a hall with four 12-metre (39¼-feet) high columns. Two other doorways led out to the eastern and southern sectors of the site. The doors were flanked by huge carved bulls and hybrid beasts – winged, human-headed bulls – a motif of kingship and power borrowed from Mesopotamia.

To the south of the gate stood the greatest building, the Apadana, an audience hall begun by Darius and completed by Xerxes. The main hall was 60 metres (197 feet) on each side, with 72 19-metre (62¼-feet) high columns holding up a roof of oak and cedar beams, imported from the Levant. The capitols of each column were carved into the shapes of animal heads. Along three sides were deep porticoes with more great columns, and huge staircases led up to the north and east façades. These still stand, and are decorated with impressive

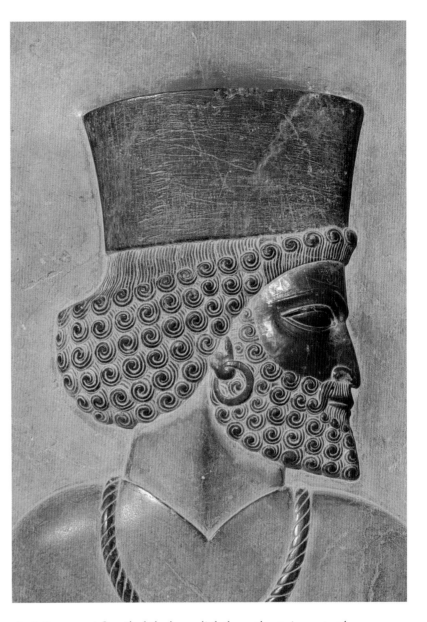

A detail of the bas reliefs from the stairway to the Apadana, showing the head of a Persian soldier, possibly one of the elite imperial guards, known as the Immortals or Apple-Bearers.

reliefs, which are among the finest surviving examples of Achaemenid art. They show 23 pairs of delegates from the nations of the empire, bringing tribute for the king (who is shown holding audience). Some of them hold barsom sheaves – bundles of sticks/grasses that had a

sacred, ceremonial purpose – and it is thought that the relief may show the celebration of the Persian New Year festival. It is interesting to note that depictions of the king at Persepolis appear to show him as much larger than his subjects, reflecting the ultimate purpose of the decoration and indeed the overall architecture of the city.

On the eastern side of the terrace sit the remains of another audience hall, known as the Hall of One Hundred Columns (also known as the Throne Hall or the Hall of Honour of the Imperial Army, the latter name referring to its later function as an imperial museum). A square hall, 70 metres (229½ feet) on each side, was filled with 100 columns. Behind it lies a lesser building, known as the Treasury, where archaeologists recovered a cache of clay tablets that proved to be records kept by financial officers (more were found in the city walls).

Side by side behind the Apadana sit two magnificent palaces. On the western side sit the remains of the palace of Darius, with suites of rooms running alongside a pillared hall. Ornate carvings show the hero king struggling with real and mythical animals. To the east of this lie the remains of Xerxes's even larger palace, and alongside it is a long building traditionally known as Xerxes's Harem, although there is no proof that this is what it was.

Pomp and Ceremony

The evidence of the site shows that Persepolis was more of a ceremonial and symbolic capital than a genuine centre of government. To begin with it was not geographically well situated in terms of the vast Persian Empire. Cities such as Babylon and Susa were closer to the main centres of population, economic activity and transport links. Persepolis was comparatively remote

A magnificent bas relief of a lion attacking a bull, from a stairway at Persepolis. This is a common motif in Persian and Mesopotamian art, and may be a symbol with astrological significance.

and inaccessible, reflected by the fact that the city was relatively unknown to the ancient Greeks until Alexander invaded the Persian Empire. The site itself shows that it was not well suited to be a major centre of population. Plumbing and sewage supply was relatively limited and there is more evidence of people living on the plain around the terrace than on the terrace itself. There is even a surviving inscription from a pillar base on the plain suggesting that Xerxes had a palace there, hinting that even when he was officially 'in residence' he stayed on the plain.

Instead it seems likely that one of the main roles of Persepolis was, on the rare occasions that the court was in residence, to function as a kind of theatre, where elaborate ceremonies drove home the magnificence and power of the king, thus asserting the legitimacy of his rule and impressing visiting dignitaries and the nobles, generals and vassals of the empire. The scale and grace of the architecture and the magnificence of the decoration backed up this message, and it is not hard to imagine the awestruck experience of a visitor to Persepolis as he made his way between huge stone beasts, mighty gateways and long avenues of giant columns, while around him the courtiers and warriors of the empire posed in all their finery.

When the court was absent, it is likely that few people actually lived on the terrace. The Treasury records indicate that around 1,300 workmen tended to the site as a sort of skeleton staff, and these men and their families probably lived in ruder structures just beyond the walls of the city.

Tombs of the Kings

Among the ceremonial functions of the city were probably those involved in the funerals of dead kings. Carved into the rocks behind the city are an unfinished tomb and two completed ones, which probably belonged to Artaxerxes II and III, late kings of the dynasty, while a few kilometres to the north of Persepolis is a more significant site where the tombs of four kings are cut into a cliffside, carved into magnificent façades. The site is called Naqsh-e Rustam – 'the picture of Rustam'. Rustam or Rostam was a Persian folk hero during the Middle Ages, by which time knowledge of the ancient Achaemenids had been largely lost, and it seems that the local people mistook the elaborate carvings for depictions of their legendary hero.

The Oxus Treasure

In fact the tombs belong to Darius the Great, Xerxes and their successors. Once, they would have been filled with stupendous treasures but they were looted (probably in ancient times) and now stand empty. It is possible, however, to get a flavour of the grave goods that might have been interred in the tombs from the Oxus Treasure, the finest surviving collection of Achaemenid artefacts. The treasure came to light in the late 19th century, when it was dug out of a hill beside the Oxus River in Central Asia, sold to merchants, stolen by bandits and then recovered by a British political officer. Eventually most of it ended up in the British Museum, London. Current thinking is that the hoard of gold and silver ornaments, figurines, jewellery, votive pieces, coins and other assorted valuables was buried to protect it from raiders, but had initially resided in a temple in Bactria, on the edge of the Achaemenid Empire, and that it was at least partly made up of pieces looted from tombs. Many of the pieces show designs similar or practically identical to reliefs at Persepolis, and it is plausible to suggest that before they were buried as grave goods or carried to Bactria, they graced the bodies and costumes of visitors to the court.

Alexander's Revenge

In 333 BCE Alexander the Great invaded the Persian Empire and three years later he was at the gates of Persepolis. According to the ancient accounts the

Macedonian king was astounded at the great wealth of the city, and he was said to have employed a baggage train of 20,000 mules and 3,000 camels to cart it away. Having looted Persepolis and occupied it for around three months, Alexander destroyed it, probably for strategic reasons (it would have been dangerous to leave a fortified city behind him).

However, ancient sources, such as Diodorus of Sicily, record a colourful tale about a drunken courtesan who goaded Alexander into burning Persepolis in revenge for the razing of the Acropolis at Athens by Xerxes during the Second Persian War, more than a century earlier.

Whatever his motives, Alexander's destructive visit marked the beginning of the end for Persepolis. Under his successors and the Second Persian Empire of the

A capital (the block atop a column) carved into the shape of a double-headed griffin. The heads are brackets and supported the architrave (a load-bearing ceiling beam). Other capitals at Persepolis took the form of bulls, lions and other symbolic creatures.

Sassanids, the locale retained its status as regional capital but probably only ever regained a fraction of its former glories, and after the Islamic conquest the city declined still further until it was completely abandoned. More recently, in 1971, the site formed the centrepiece of extravagant celebrations of the 2,500th anniversary of the Iranian monarchy, with a tent city constructed to house heads of state and other guests attending a lavish ceremony there.

BABYLON

LOCATION: EUPHRATES RIVER, SOUTH OF BAGHDAD, IRAQ

DATE OF CONSTRUCTION: BEFORE 2400 BCE

ABANDONED: c 1ST CENTURY CE

BUILT BY: BABYLONIANS

KEY FEATURES: CITY WALLS; ISHTAR GATE; PROCESSIONAL WAY; ETEMENANKI ZIGGURAT; ESAGIL TEMPLE; HANGING GARDENS

A city of such greatness and magnificence that its name and repute have far outlived its physical fabric, Babylon was by turns the capital of the world, the largest city in the world and the possible site of one of the wonders of the ancient world. It was a place of magic and learning, exile and sadness, power and glory, which has left an indelible mark on global culture even as it crumbles into dust at an accelerating rate.

Situated on the banks of the Euphrates about 80 kilometres (50 miles) south of modern Baghdad, Babylon was a great city for nearly two millennia, yet was effectively abandoned by the start of the Common Era. Though probably not among the very oldest of the Mesopotamian city-states, Babylon already existed during the Akkadian period of Sumerian civilization and is first mentioned in a tablet from the reign of Shar-kali-sharri of Akkad (possibly as early as the 23th century BCE, depending on the chronology used).

City of the Law-giver

Babylon first rose to prominence and power under the Babylonian king Hammurabi, who ruled from 1792–1750 BCE, establishing what is now known as the Old Babylonian kingdom. Under Hammurabi, Babylon grew to magnificence, becoming probably the largest city in the world. Temples, shrines and public buildings multiplied and the city acquired massive walls. Hammurabi is best known today for his Code, among the oldest set of laws known to mankind, which were inscribed on large stelae written in Akkadian, the day-to-day language of the Babylonians at this time, and displayed in public for all to see.

The Old Babylonian kingdom was short-lived and was soon conquered by first the Hittites and then the Kassites. However, the city itself remained the regional capital for several centuries until suffering declining fortunes during the early 1st millennium BCE, with climate fluctuations, famine, plague and the depredations of nomadic raiders taking their toll. Meanwhile, the Assyrians to the north grew in power until Babylon fell under their sway around 800 BCE.

The city both benefited and suffered from their attentions. On the one hand Babylon was of central religious, political and strategic importance, and the Assyrians were able to bolster their hegemony over the region by renewing and enlarging it, but on the

An Iraqi reconstruction of the Ishtar Gate. Most of the remains of the original were removed from Babylon by the archaeologist Robert Koldewey, and used in a reconstruction at Berlin's Pergamon Museum. Other elements can be found in museums around the world.

other they struggled constantly to suppress the rebellious Babylonians. In 689 BCE the Assyrian king, Sennacherib, sacked the city and had it razed to the ground, but just a few decades later the Assyrian Empire collapsed and King Nabopolassar established a Neo-Babylonian dynasty that reached its apogee under his son, Nebuchadnezzar (reign 604–562 BCE).

Nebuchadnezzar and the Hanging Gardens

Under Nebuchadnezzar the city reached its greatest magnificence, as its population climbed above the 200,000 mark – the first city in human history to do so. Nebuchadnezzar enlarged the empire as far as the shores of the Mediterranean, conquering Israel and Judah and deporting the Jews to his capital, where they joined nations and peoples from every corner of the Earth. He engaged in an extensive series of works, enlarging the city, strengthening its walls, rebuilding its temples and ziggurat, and building vast palaces, citadels, ornate gates and magnificent processional ways. For his wife, homesick for the lush vegetation of her homeland, he reputedly built a series of hanging gardens (i.e. gardens arrayed on stepped balconies or terraces) that sat atop a great hall and were watered by a ceaseless cascade mechanically extracted from the river.

This Neo-Babylonian Empire was also short-lived, falling to the Achaemenid Persians under Cyrus in 539 BCE. According to the account of the ancient Greek historian Herodotus, Cyrus breached the city's mighty walls with a brilliant stratagem. The only weak spots in the fortifications were where the Euphrates flowed through them, so Cyrus stationed troops at these spots and diverted the river into the basin for long enough for his armies to march up the dry bed and into the city. Supposedly the city was so huge that those in the centre had no idea the Persians had breached the walls and were surprised in the middle of celebrating a festival.

Under the Achaemenids the city continued to be a religious, administrative and cultural centre, and when Alexander the Great conquered it in 331 BCE he seemed intent on preserving its role. He renovated parts of the city, added buildings, including a theatre, and encouraged commerce, arts and the sciences, but his death not long after – in Nebuchadnezzar's own palace – spelt doom for Babylon. The fragile empire he had so quickly forged fell apart just as rapidly, as his generals fought for control of the different regions. As the effective capital of the world, Babylon found itself at the centre of a series of wars that steadily depleted its material and human resources. Mass deportations, such as one recorded in a tablet of 275 BCE, further diminished the failing city's population and the city finally died with a whimper at some point during the hegemony of the Parthian Empire, which ruled Mesopotamia until the 3rd century CE.

Rediscovering Babylon

By the dawn of the Common Era Babylon was largely deserted, its lavish monuments and edifices reduced to piles of crumbling bricks or buried beneath dust. Although its location was not forgotten and its name retained legendary and biblical connotations, there was little evidence of its former glories. Without constant maintenance of the system of irrigation canals that made the area agriculturally viable, even the ecosystem changed and the area became a dusty, arid plain.

This never before published drawing by Andrew George shows a remarkable stone stela commemorating the completion of Babylon's ziggurat by Nebuchadnezzar II in about 590 BCE. The monument's relief depicts Nebuchadnezzar alongside the Etemenanki, and its inscription records the king's good works.
No other contemporary depiction of the ziggurat or of Nebuchadnezzar has survived, let alone of the two together. The monument is now in the Schøyen Collection, Norway.

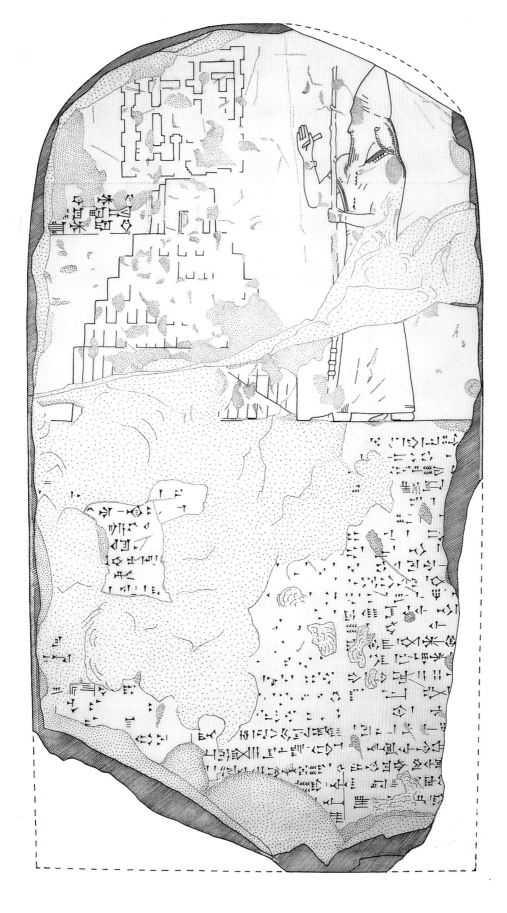

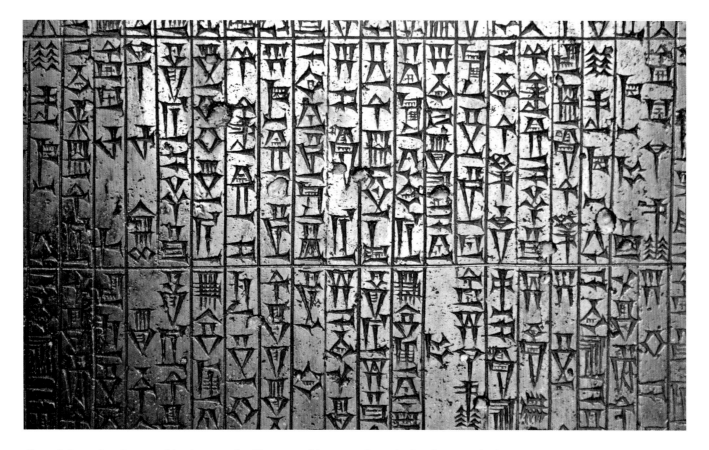

One of the stelae (stone tablets) set up by Hammurabi c 1760 BCE, to display his Code.

When European travellers once again began to frequent the region, all that remained were a number of tells – mounds built up as generations occupied the same site for millennia. One of the tells was even called the 'Babil'. Armed with copies of Herodotus and other ancient writers, gentlemen adventurers sought to relate the barren mounds to the Classical accounts, but not until the methodical excavations of the Deutsche-Orient Gesellschaft (German-Orient Society), led by Dr Robert Koldewey and carried out from 1899–1917, was the ancient city properly rediscovered. The city that Koldewey's team painstakingly uncovered was essentially Nebuchadnezzar's Babylon. They traced its walls, palaces and temples, and even identified the possible inspirations for the legendary Tower of Babel and Hanging Gardens.

Rough Guide to Babylon

Ancient Babylon was roughly rectangular in shape, oriented on a SW-NE angle, split in two by the Euphrates about a third of the way in from the west. The most significant locations were on the eastern side. A huge wall ran around the entire city. Herodotus famously claimed that it was so wide that there was room enough on top for 'a four-horse chariot to run'. In fact Koldewey discovered that it was even wider than this – between the outer face of burned brick and the inner one of crude, dried mud bricks, and atop the layer of rubble that filled the space between, ran a broad roadway up to 30 metres (98½ feet) wide – room enough for two chariots to pass. The wall was studded with great towers at regular intervals and stretched for 18 kilometres (11¼ miles), while the city covered an area of 8.5 square kilometres (3¼ square miles), making it the largest of the ancient Mesopotamian cities. According to

Herodotus, the walls were nearly 100 metres (328 feet) high, and on the eastern side of the city they were further enhanced by a deep moat. Straddling the wall just to the east of the Euphrates, where it entered the city's northern precincts, the Tell Babil marked the site of Nebuchadnezzar's summer palace/fortress.

Perhaps the most impressive find was the Ishtar Gate, a ceremonial entrance to the city created by Nebuchadnezzar to strike awe into the hearts of visitors. They were presented with a high arch spanning the gap between two mighty 25-metre (82-feet) high towers decorated with brightly coloured glazed tiles and reliefs of fearsome dragons, lions and bulls, all raised on a platform 15 metres (49¼ feet) above ground level. The gate now resides in Berlin's Pergamon Museum. Leading from the Ishtar Gate into the heart of the city, Koldewey traced the course of a processional way 20 metres (65½ feet) wide, also lined with glazed tiles and reliefs of lions. This formed the main axis of the city, and ran parallel to the river, past palaces and temples, until reaching a street that ran off to the left, towards the river, and which passed between the two central structures of Babylon – the Etemenanki and the Esagil.

The Axis Mundi

The Etemenanki (meaning 'the house that is the foundation of heaven and Earth') was a ziggurat, or stepped tower, which represented – in a very literal fashion for the Babylonians – the *axis mundi* or axis of the world. This was the place where the different parts of the Babylonian cosmos, including the heavens, the earthly plane and the palace of the gods, came together, and where creation itself had begun. The Etemenanki ziggurat may well have been the basis for the legend of the Tower of Babel. At its base it was 91 metres (295 feet) square, with a broad staircase ascending its seven stages, but it cannot be said for sure how tall it was (although the ancient tradition was that it stood as tall as its base was wide).

The Esagil was the temple of Marduk, the tutelary deity of Babylon and the leader of the Babylonian pantheon. Here dwelt the idol of Marduk – a golden statue that represented the actual presence of the god in ceremonies – together with the idols of deities from other city-states within Babylon's sphere of influence.

Other features discovered by Koldewey included the throne room of Nebuchadnezzar, a 50-metre (164-feet) long room magnificently decorated with coloured glazed bricks and reliefs showing lions and trees of life, and a series of underground chambers with barrel-vaulted roofs, asphalt waterproofing and a system of wells. Koldewey was convinced that 'a mechanic hydraulic machine stood there, which worked on the same principle as our chain pump', and that he had discovered the site of the Hanging Gardens of Babylon. He supposed that the gardens had been laid out on the terraced roof of the building and watered via the mechanical hydraulic system, with the running water and shading vegetation cooling the hall below, where the business of the court took place. Modern archaeological opinion is divided, however, and the city of Nineveh is said by some to be a more likely location for the legendary gardens, if they existed at all.

Modern Babylon

More recently Babylon has become a figurative and literal battleground in the Gulf conflicts. Following on from Nebuchadnezzar, whose rebuilding of Babylon was a statement of power and a tool for legitimizing his rule, and who had the millions of bricks used stamped with his name and a proclamation of his glory, Saddam Hussein attempted something similar. In 1985 he started reconstructing the city with bricks stamped 'This was built by Saddam Hussein, son of Nebuchadnezzar, to glorify Iraq'. More recently, US forces have occupied and landscaped the area and their helicopters, trucks, earthmovers and troops have been blamed for significant damage to the ruins and the archaeological record.

PETRA

LOCATION: SOUTHERN JORDAN

DATE OF CONSTRUCTION: *c* 2ND CENTURY BCE

ABANDONED: *c* 6TH CENTURY CE

BUILT BY: NABATAEANS

KEY FEATURES: SIQ GORGE; ROCK-HEWN BUILDINGS;
URN-TOMBS; THE TREASURY; AMPHITHEATRE; BYZANTINE
CHURCH AND MOSAICS

One of the great monuments of world heritage and recently voted one of the new Seven Wonders of the World, Petra is a unique and beautiful ancient city with biblical roots that grew to become one of the greatest trading centres in the world. Yet amazingly it was all but lost, except to fable, rumour and occasional nomadic residents, for 700 years.

'It is impossible to conceive of any thing more awe-ful [*sic*] or sublime than such an approach,' wrote two Royal Navy captains, Irby and Mangles, in 1868, describing their visit to Petra, and in particular their experience of one of the great sights the world has to offer: the appearance at the end of a dark, narrow gorge of a mighty classical frontage carved into the living rock, shaded with many hues of pink, orange and red, bathed in vivid desert sunlight. (The famous colours of Petra are down to iron-rich water percolating through porous sandstone and depositing its mineral load.)

Visitors approaching Petra by the Siq (Arabic for the 'shaft'), a winding gorge over 1.6 kilometres (1 mile) long and 60 metres (197 feet) deep, but at times just 3–4 metres (10–13 feet) wide, come face to face with a building known as Al-Khazneh (the Treasury), which is 33 metres (108 feet) wide and 40 metres (131 feet) high, with great pillars, pediments, porticoes and statues, carved directly into the cliff face. From here the gorge continues northeastwards past more façades, bends north at a great Roman-style amphitheatre and eventually opens out onto a broad valley studded with ruins and dotted with yet more enormous tombs carved into the rock. These are the remains of Petra, the Greek name for the city, which means, simply, 'the Rock'. To its inhabitants it was known as Raqmu or Reqem.

Half as Old as Time

Petra was the capital of the ancient Nabataean civilization, which flowered into a Golden Age around the 2nd and 1st centuries BCE, but with roots much further back in time. In its prime it was the junction of the world's main trade routes linking East to West, a clearing house for caravans bringing silks and other goods from China via the Silk Road to be exchanged for the produce of Rome and the Mediterranean world. Cunning hydrological engineering and husbandry of resources allowed the Nabataeans to create an artificial oasis at Petra, so that a great city, renowned from Carthage to China, could flourish in the midst of a barren desert region. It is now known, thanks in part to a heavy marketing

Al-Khazneh, the Treasury, a rock-hewn tomb that confronts visitors approaching via the gorge. According to legend, the giant urn conceals treasure, hence the building's name.

campaign by the Jordanian tourist authorities, as 'the rose-red city, half as old as time', a couplet from an 1845 poem by clergyman John William Burgon.

The region has been occupied since the Stone Age and it is likely that the dramatic setting and geology of the place, with its unfailing springs and narrow canyons gouged into the base of an imposing mountain (Jabal Haroun, or Aaron's Mount, said to be the resting place of Aaron, brother of Moses), made it both religiously and militarily significant from prehistoric times onwards. Deposits of copper ore also made it a centre of early metallurgy with the dawn of the Bronze Age. The earliest records of the people who dwelt here come from the Old Testament, with references to tribes such as the Horites, and later Semitic peoples such as the Edomites and Amorites (see box on page 39).

The Wealth of Nations

At this time the famous buildings of Petra did not exist. It was probably a tent city, originally occupied only on an irregular, seasonal basis by large groups of nomads. The Bronze Age saw the rise of 'super-powers', such as Egypt, Sumer and the Hittites, and a corresponding development of trade. Petra was situated at a crucial juncture of trade routes between Egypt, the Levant and Mesopotamia. The long valley that ran from the Sea of Galilee to the Dead Sea (the Jordan Valley) and then on down to the Gulf of Aqaba and the Red Sea (the Wadi Arabah), formed a natural highway for trade from what would later become the port of Ezion-Geber (now Aqaba) all the way up to Damascus, Palmyra and the Phoenician ports – this route came to be known as the King's Highway. Petra was right next to the Wadi Arabah.

Meanwhile the route from the Euphrates-Tigris delta across the Arabian deserts to Egypt and the Levant also passed through Petra, where it split into the road across the Sinai to Luxor and later Alexandria, and across the

Negev to Gaza, gateway to the Mediterranean. Yet another major trade route led up from Aden at the tip of the Arabian peninsula, along the eastern shore of the Red Sea, to Petra. Maritime trade was still extremely limited by primitive naval technology, so the land routes were pre-eminent. Later they would become even more important, as this Mesopotamian-Mediterranean trade network was plugged into the continent-spanning Silk Road, which disgorged the wealth of the Orient by sea to ports such as Basra (at the mouth of the Euphrates-Tigris), Aden and Ezion-Geber, and via the land routes further north.

At first Petra proved a handy stronghold for the desert tribes who would raid these rich caravans. Later these tribes would extract tribute for allowing safe-passage and offering protection from other raiders. Still later, they would develop into a trading hub, offering supplies, fresh mounts, services etc., in return making money from taxes and tariffs, and eventually becoming merchants. Petra would go on to win important trading monopolies, such as the lucrative bitumen trade and the fabulously wealthy trade in frankincense (an aromatic resin worth more by weight than gold).

As trade increased, so did the strategic and economic importance of Petra, and regional powers vied for control. For instance, Egyptian documents of the early 12th century BCE record pharaonic triumphs over the people of Seir, which was probably a reference to Petra, and by this time the region had been under the hegemony of the Egyptians for many centuries. The earliest recorded kings of Petra date to the 8th century BCE, although several biblical figures, such as Rekem and Balaam, mentioned in Genesis and probably dating to around 1300 BCE, may have filled this role. The establishment of the kingdom of Israel, c 1000 BCE, saw a period of constant warfare between the Hebrews and their Semitic neighbours, including the Petrans, leading the latter to cheer the subjugation of Israel by the Babylonians

under Nebuchadnezzar in 586 BCE. They thus earned the undying enmity of the Hebrews, as expressed through a range of colourful and vitriolic curses called down by various Old Testament prophets (see box on page 39).

The Nabataeans

Around this period the Edomites who inhabited Petra gave way to the Nabataeans, a nomadic tribe from northern Arabia descended, according to a now discredited tradition, from Nebaioth, son of Ishmael, who was the son of Abraham. Egyptian and Persian power in the region had given way to Alexander the Great in the 4th century BCE, and his successors, the

The Monastery, the largest tomb façade in Petra, measures 50 metres (164 feet) across and 45 metres (148 feet) high. It dates to the 1st century BCE and was dedicated to the deified Nabatean king Obodas.

Ptolemies and Antigonids, battled for control of Petra for 200 years. Eventually, however, both these empires declined and in the power vacuum the Nabataeans flourished. Careful hydrological engineering, including the excavation of a great cistern to capture the infrequent flash floods that inundated the dry wadis, allowed them to sustain large-scale agriculture and provide valuable resources for the trans-desert caravans.

Combined with their control of the trade routes, the Nabataeans grew rich and powerful, minting coins and developing a script that would later become Arabic, now used across much of the Muslim world. During this Golden Age the city began to take shape.

The earliest rock-carved tombs probably pre-dated the Nabataeans, but these are relatively crude. As they became settled and wealthy the Nabataeans began to build freestanding monumental architecture and to excavate magnificent tombs from the sandstone cliffs and mountainsides, with the primary building boom, including construction of the most famous rock-cut tombs, taking place around the end of the 1st century BCE. At first their style was mainly borrowed from the Ptolemaic Egyptians, and later Greek influences took root. Idiosyncratic Nabataean touches include the prevalence of urns atop the rock-cut tomb facades. Many of the buildings would have had lush gardens, while the gorge and valley floors would have been crowded with less permanent wooden structures.

Cave tombs. Despite an official ban on using the structures as houses, some of these tombs are still used by local Bedouin as homes.

Later History of Petra

The rise of Rome saw Petra fall into the Roman sphere of influence. Petran princes served with Roman armies and may have belonged to the Roman jet set. Roman custom often saw client-kings cede their states to Rome on their demise and in 106 CE, with the death of the last Nabataean king, Rabbel II, Petra passed into Roman control. Although the city survived as the capital of Arabia Petraea, the most prosperous of all Roman provinces (at one time it produced a quarter of the economic output of the entire empire), the seeds of Petra's decline had already been sown. Advances in naval technology saw more ship-borne trade, while the land routes increasingly followed Roman roads that bypassed Petra altogether.

The city lingered on as a religious centre until the Islamic conquest. Pre-Christian Nabataean beliefs and religious life remain relatively obscure and open to speculation. Their main god was a solar deity named Dushara, and according to some of the more speculative interpretations of the evidence he was accompanied by a mother-goddess and resurrected son to form a trinity that may have had a strong influence on nascent Christianity (it should be noted that this is very much a fringe theory). Under the Byzantine Empire (from the 4th century CE) Petra became a centre of Christianity, with a Byzantine church, the incredible mosaic floors of which can still be seen. By the time of the Islamic conquest Petra was a largely deserted city, damaged by severe earthquakes and without a raison d'être. It had a brief resurgence as an important military site in Crusader times, when a fort was built on one of the high points overlooking the main valley, but under the Ottomans it was neglected.

By the 19th century Petra was the preserve of the nomadic Bedouin tribespeople and the region was hostile to travellers, especially non-Muslims. But memory of the exotic and striking city in the mountain had lingered on in the West and in 1812 Swiss explorer Johann Ludwig Burckhardt determined to visit the site. Disguised as an

THE MOST CURSED CITY

While the archaeological evidence suggests that Petra did not exist in early Biblical times, the Bible tells a different story, in which the fractious relationship between the Edomites of Petra and the ancient Hebrews led the prophets of Israel to call down a battery of curses on the Petrans, making it the most cursed place in the Bible. Moses was the first to curse it, but the vitriol really began to flow when the Petrans gloated over the 1st millennium BCE Assyrian and Babylonian conquests of Israel and the subsequent travails of the Hebrews. Isaiah, Jeremiah and Ezekiel all invoked curses of desolation and waste. Isaiah had some particularly harsh words, '...the Lord has doomed [the Petrans], has given them over for slaughter... their land shall be soaked with their blood, and their soil made rich with their fat...'

Egyptian sheikh, speaking fluent Arabic and so well versed in Islam that he was recognized as an expert on Sharia law, Burckhardt pretended to be a pious Muslim pilgrim hoping to sacrifice a goat at the tomb of the prophet Aaron. This was dangerous territory – six years earlier a German explorer, Ulrich Seetzen, had tried a similar ruse and been murdered. With the aid of a local guide, however, Burckhardt penetrated the Siq and became the first European to gaze on the wonders of Petra for 700 years. Six years later Captains Irby and Mangle followed in his footsteps, accompanied by an artist, and in 1826 a French architect and explorer, Léon de Laborde, carried out the first systematic survey of the ruins. Their writings and pictures caused a sensation – Petra was back on the world stage. Today it is probably the biggest tourist attraction in Jordan and continues to be the subject of intensive archaeological study.

TROY

LOCATION: DARDANELLES, TURKEY
DATE OF CONSTRUCTION: *c* 2600 BCE
ABANDONED: ROMAN TIMES
BUILT BY: TROJANS? SUB-KINGDOM OF HITTITE EMPIRE?
KEY FEATURES: NUMEROUS PHASES OF OCCUPATION;
MASSIVE WALLS AND CITADEL; TREASURE OF PRIAM

For the ancient Greeks and Romans there was no doubt that Troy was a real place and that the epics of Homer were genuine records of history, but with the rise of critical history in the modern era, Troy was consigned to the realm of legend. The pioneering and controversial work of Heinrich Schliemann changed that and today Troy is again the site of fierce battles, this time of a purely academic nature, concerning the historicity of Homer.

The mainstay of Greek literature, and by extension a foundation stone of the Western canon, was the cycle of epic poems about the Achaean (Bronze Age Greek) expedition to Troy, and the many heroes, gods, battles and adventures associated with it. The only complete survivors of these epics are Homer's *Iliad* and *Odyssey*, but these give a clear picture of a great city situated on a hill near the mouth of the River Scamander in a region known as Troas (modern-day Çanakkale in Turkey), a city known both as Troy and as Ilion. Legendary Troy commanded the trade routes between the Aegean and the Black Sea via the Straits of the Dardanelles, and ruled over the surrounding lands from behind its apparently unbreachable walls. According to various Greek myths and traditions, the Trojans descended from Achaean stock.

Ancient Greek historians dated the decade-long Trojan War to between the 14th and 12th centuries BCE, most popularly to 1193–1183 BCE, at the culmination of which Troy was destroyed and the Trojans scattered, their lands eventually occupied by later immigrants. To the Greeks of Homer's age (the 8th century BCE) the ruins of the ancient city were still visible and the remnants of the walls may even have been used for protection by the small remaining community. Alexander the Great visited it in 334 BCE and the Roman emperor Augustus founded a city there, called Novum Ilium (New Troy), which flourished for 300 years but declined under the Byzantine Empire. By the time of the Islamic conquest, the city was deserted and the location lost. Thanks to Homer, ancient Troy was never forgotten, but as European intellectuals began to develop a more critical approach to history after the Enlightenment, it was assumed that the stories were little more than myths.

'The Second Destroyer'

One man who disagreed was German businessman and amateur archaeologist Heinrich Schliemann. Fascinated by Troy since he was a little boy, Schliemann had made a fortune trading in Russia and America and decided to devote himself to tracking down proof of Homer's historicity (whether or not the events, people and places Homer wrote about really happened/existed). Homer's epics contain specific geographical information and although the coastline in the region has changed over the millennia (see below) some of these clues pointed to a mound near a village called Hissarlik. In 1870 Schliemann started digging and quickly discovered that the mound concealed evidence of several ancient cities built on top of one another, in successive phases of occupation.

Convinced that he had found the site of Troy, but with little patience for the painstaking methods of conventional archaeology, Schliemann had his workmen dig a trench right down to the lowest and oldest phase, which he assumed must be the original Troy of Homer. In doing

Some of the best-preserved ruins at Troy, these walls
mark the main entrance to the site for most tour parties.
They probably belong to the settlement phase known as
Troy VI, or possibly Troy VII.

so he ploughed through no fewer than eight other phases of occupation, doing so much damage that some contemporaries called him 'the second destroyer of Troy'. In Schliemann's defence, many other archaeologists of the time were just as bad, and some contemporary experts argue that he has been unfairly vilified.

Eventually Schliemann decided that the penultimate phase of occupation, labelled Troy II (Troy I being the oldest and IX the youngest), which had massive stone walls and towers and grand public buildings, must be the city of Priam and Paris. A layer of ash separating this phase from the next indicated that the city had perished in fire, matching Homer's description of the fiery demise of Troy.

Reports of Schliemann's discovery captured global attention, but the best was yet to come. In 1873,

according to his own account, he unearthed a bronze vessel from the walls of a building he assumed to be Priam's palace, which proved to contain a fabulous treasure of gold and silver, including exotic head-dresses and beads, plates and drinking vessels. Smuggled to Greece and revealed to the world in 1874, Priam's Treasure, as Schliemann was quick to label it, caused a sensation and forever changed the public perception of archaeology, introducing an element of romance, adventure and treasure hunting.

Schliemann's shady dealings with the treasure caused problems with the Turkish authorities, and the archaeologists who succeeded him discovered that some of his primary conclusions were off the mark. Troy II was quickly identified as an early Bronze Age town dating back to 2600–2250 BCE, more than a thousand years before the supposed time of Priam. The other phases of note were Troy VI – a high Bronze Age citadel with huge walls and palace-like buildings and Troy VII, its successor, which are considered much more likely candidates for the Homeric Troy (although Schliemann would never have seen the walls, as he was excavating in the centre of the mound and they ran around the edges). Troy IX was Novum Ilium, the city founded by the Romans.

Troy II

Schliemann may have been wrong about Troy II's age, but it was an important and impressive settlement nonetheless. It was a fortified citadel with walls of stone blocks and mud bricks, with regular towers and massive gate-houses, one approached by a wide stone ramp. Within the walls were two large public spaces, one of them colonnaded and leading to a grand building of stone and mud brick known as the Megaron, comparable with Mycenaean palaces in Greece from a thousand years later, with a colonnaded porch giving onto a great hall with a huge hearth. It was probably the hall of the settlement's chief. Together with the treasures discovered by Schliemann, these findings show that Troy II was extremely wealthy. Evidence of textile industry suggests one source of the wealth, while the settlement's strategic location with regard to the trade routes through the Dardanelles suggests another, also attested to by extensive evidence of trade links with the wider Mediterranean world, such as pottery and imported metals.

Troy VI

The most impressive ruins at the site are from the phase named Troy VI, which dates to the mid-2nd millennium BCE. Imposing fortifications, with massive walls of dressed limestone blocks topped with mud bricks, over 4 metres (13¼ feet) thick, and five gates protected by high towers, encircled a citadel area containing concentric rings of large buildings on mounting terraces. Some of these buildings are two storeys high, made of wood and bricks on stone foundations, and may have been palaces or mansions. Clearly Troy VI was a centre of economic and military importance, although the fortified area was more of a citadel than a

---

A fanciful reconstruction of the wooden horse of Troy. According to the epic cycle, the Greeks grew weary of their decade-long siege of Troy and arrived upon the clever ruse of hiding troops in a huge wooden horse left on their departure as an apparent offering to placate the gods, based, according to one theory, on an ancient custom whereby a defeated general surrendered his horse. The horse was taken inside the city walls by the jubilant Trojans and, that same night, the Greek troops climbed down from their hideout and destroyed the city. The Trojan Horse is only briefly mentioned in Homer's Odyssey, *which describes a 'horse of wood, which Epeius made with Athena's help, the horse which once Odysseus led up into the citadel as a thing of guile, when he had filled it with the men who sacked Ilium [Troy].' It is detailed more fully in Virgil's* Aeneid, *which describes 'a steed of monstrous height' with 'sides planked with pine'.*

The amphitheatre from the Roman phase of settlement at Troy, when it was known as Novum Ilium (Troy IX in the archaeological record). The Roman city was founded after the Greek city on the site was destroyed in 85 BCE, during the time of Sulla. It flourished for several centuries but was eventually abandoned sometime in the 5th century CE.

city. In 1988, however, further excavations revealed evidence of city ramparts enclosing a much larger area, allowing space for up to 10,000 inhabitants.

So was Troy VI the Troy of Homer? For a while it was thought likely, but Troy VI probably dates to 1800–1300 BCE, outside most of the traditional dates ascribed to Homeric Troy. More importantly, there are none of the tell-tale signs of war or siege, such as ash from fires,

buried stores or treasure, goods abandoned by fleeing residents or the skeletons of those killed violently. The city was probably destroyed by an earthquake.

Troy VIIa

Many of the signs of war are present in the next phase of occupation, known as Troy VIIa (because it is the first of several sub-phases of occupation). Troy VIIa was essentially the same city as Troy VI, apparently reoccupied and partially rebuilt after the earthquake. The evidence suggests that conditions had changed, however, with some of the grand mansions of the earlier phase now subdivided for multiple occupancy and the damaged fortifications of previous eras merely patched up, rather than enlarged/improved as past generations of Trojans had done. The new buildings were more densely packed and smaller (possibly indicating that people who used to live in the wider metropolis were now crowded into the citadel for safety).

Evidence suggestive of warfare and siege is present. Many houses have storage pits for large clay jars built into their floors, possibly for supplies in case of siege (although this may also have been normal practice), and some unburied skeletons have been found. Most significantly, the demise of the city is marked with a layer of ash. Troy VIIa dates to around 1250 BCE, and although there is significant debate over the exact date of its destruction, it was probably around 1200 BCE, similar to Classical Greek dating of the Trojan War.

Wilusa of the Hittites

Important evidence apparently linking the city at Hissarlik to Homer's epics comes from the records of the Hittites, the civilization under whose remit the region of Troas would have fallen in the late 13th century BCE. Hittite texts mention the place-names Wilusa and Taruisa. Mycenaean Greeks used a 'w' letter that later Greeks dropped, and evidence from the meter used in the composition of the *Iliad* suggests that Ilion was originally Willion, probably a derivation of Wilusa. Taruisa, meanwhile, is lexically linked to Troas and Troy. Other texts describe features of Wilusa, such as a water tunnel, which conform to archaeological findings at Hissarlik. Hittite diplomatic letters mention an incident involving Wilusa and aggression by a nation called the Ahhiyawa, possibly a Hittite version of the Achaeans.

Homer's Troy?

Troy VIIa thus seems like the most likely candidate as the true Homeric city, but there is controversy over whether the evidence really points to this conclusion, and even over whether there is any historical accuracy to the epics. The Hittite textual evidence is circumstantial and there is no direct evidence linking the site at Hissarlik to Wilusa or the place-names Ilion or Troy. In fact, some scholars suggest that there never was a city called Troy and that the ancients mistook the name of a region (Troas) for the name of a city.

What about Homer's apparent accuracy regarding the geography of Troy/Hissarlik? Recent research on the ancient coastline of the area (before sedimentation) suggests that it closely matches Homer's description, as do other features of Hissarlik. But this could simply reflect the fact that Homer travelled to the area before composing his epics. The Greeks had not long before settled nearby areas, and it is possible that they sought out a place to which they could attach pre-existing legends and folklore about ancient battles. So the city at Hissarlik, which would have been little more than a relic community living amid ruins in Homer's time, might have become retrospectively identified as Troy.

If Homer was right, the Achaeans who destroyed Troy were Bronze Age Greeks i.e. Mycenaeans. Certainly the linguistic evidence of the epics suggests that they derive from Mycenaean legends and traditions, but there is no evidence linking the destruction of Troy VIIa (or any other phases) to the Mycenaeans. In fact, archaeologists believe that at the period in question, around 1200 BCE, the Mycenaeans might well have been preoccupied with the collapse of their civilization in its heartland in Greece, where most of their major cities seem to have been destroyed at around this time.

Ultimately it may be fruitless to attempt to draw specific correspondences between the Homeric epics – which are literary fictions based on ancient oral traditions – and a real place, let alone to try to prove the existence of Homeric characters through archaeological investigation of a site that is more than 4,000 years old. What the excavations at Hissarlik do prove is that this was the site of an important city for 2,000 years, the centre of a fascinating culture about which we still know very little.

PERGAMUM

LOCATION: NORTHWESTERN TURKEY, NEAR THE AEGEAN COAST

DATE OF CONSTRUCTION: *c* 300 BCE

ABANDONED: *c* 8TH CENTURY CE

BUILT BY: ATTALID GREEKS

KEY FEATURES: ACROPOLIS; ALTAR OF ZEUS; LIBRARY OF PERGAMUM; ASKLEPIEION; AMPHITHEATRE; TRAJANEUM; RED BASILICA; STATUARY AND FRIEZES

Renowned as the most graceful and cultural city of its era, the city of Pergamum was famed for the scholarship of its library, the artistic achievements of its architects and sculptors, the enlightened model of its governance and the medical and therapeutic powers of its great Asklepieion. Historically it bridged the divide between Classical Greece and the age of Rome.

Pergamum, also spelt Pergamom and Pergamon, was an ancient Greek city-state in Mysia, in northwestern Anatolia (modern-day Turkey), which came to rival Athens and Alexandria as centres of Hellenistic achievement and renown. The city was based around an acropolis built on a 355-metre (1,165-feet) high spur between two tributaries of the River Caicus (today known as Bakırçay), not far inland from the Aegean. It was a minor settlement until the early 3rd century BCE, when Lysimachus made it a fortress for the safeguarding of his treasury. Lysimachus had been one of Alexander the Great's generals and had taken control of Anatolia following the great man's death, contending with Seleucus of Syria for control of Asia Minor. When Lysimachus was killed by his eastern rival in 281 BCE (at the battle of Corupedium), Philataerus, the man he had appointed to control the fortress, seized control of the treasure and established a power base at Pergamum.

The Attalids

Philataerus established the Attalid dynasty, named after his father Attalus. His successor, Eumenes, secured the city, but it was his nephew Attalus I (269–197 BCE) who achieved eternal renown for Pergamum by defeating the Galatians – Celts from Thrace who had crossed over to Asia Minor in 278 BCE and terrorized the Greek states of the region with decades of raids and plundering. Most rulers bought them off with tribute, but Attalus I refused to pay, instead destroying the Celtic armies in a great battle. The famous sculpture known as *The Dying Gaul* was originally erected at Pergamum as a monument to this victory. Hailed as the saviour of Greek Asia Minor, Attalus took the name 'Soter' ('Saviour') and declared himself king. He also forged close links with the rising power to the west – Rome.

His son, Eumenes II, who ruled from 197–159 BCE, engaged in a major programme of building and established Pergamum as one of the pre-eminent cities in the Greek world – a new Athens in architectural, cultural and political terms. Its population increased to over 200,000. Later rulers gained power through close alliances with Rome, eventually gaining control of most of Asia Minor.

The ruins of the Acropolis at Pergamum, with the Trajaneum in the foreground.

Roman Pergamum

Attalus III had no heir and to avoid civil conflict over the succession he bequeathed the kingdom to Rome. Upon his death in 133 BCE, Pergamum became a Roman possession. But with the Romans distracted by domestic political issues, a local prince named Aristonicus, an illegitimate son of Eumenes II, made a bid for power with the backing of the slave and serf classes, in what has been described as one of the first attempts at a popular revolution. Declaring himself Eumenes III, he promised to establish a state called Heliopolis where all would live free, but he was defeated by a Roman army and taken back to Rome to be executed.

Pergamum passed into Roman control, but on the whole the Romans respected Pergamene property and autonomy, making the city the capital of the province of Asia Minor. In recognition of its influence and status the city was granted permission to build temples to the imperial cult, including ones in honour of Augustus and Trajan. It continued to flourish under the Roman aegis for several centuries, maintaining its reputation as a centre for academia and education, arts and architecture, and healing and medicine. The city declined under the Byzantines but was still inhabited by the time of the Arab invasion in the 8th century CE.

The Acropolis

The site of most of the important buildings of Pergamum was the acropolis, extending down the sides of the steep central hill, which was cut into a series of artificial terraces. At the top were the king's palaces and the arsenals (barracks and military storehouses). Descending the hill from west to east, lower terraces housed the *temenos* or sacred precinct, which included temples to the Roman emperors, then the famous library (see below) and its associated Sanctuary of Athena, then the Altar of Zeus (see below) and below that the *agora* (forum/marketplace). In front of these, facing south over the plain and still dominating the prospect of the city today, a great amphitheatre with seating for 10,000 people was cut into the steep hillside. Next to it was a temple to Dionysus, god of wine and entertainment, while running along its base was a giant *stoa* (pillared portico) 247 metres (810 feet) long. Other features of the Acropolis include the *heroons* or royal tombs, and the Propylea or monumental gate.

Below the acropolis was a gymnasium – a centre for the physical, intellectual and moral training of the city's youth. Measuring 200 x 150 metres (656 x 492 feet), it was the largest gymnasium in the Greek world, reflecting the importance of education to the Attalids (they also sponsored educational establishments in other Greek cities as a way of boosting their profile and status). It had three levels, each assigned to a different age group, with exercise yards, a lecture hall, its own library, baths and a temple. From the lower levels of the city a sacred way ran off to the southwest, towards the Asklepieion (see below).

The Altar and Other Temples

Pergamum hosted temples to the cult of Augustus (the first Roman emperor, who courted considerable controversy back home by allowing himself to be deified during his own lifetime) and Trajan. His temple, the Trajaneum, a white marble building with 54 columns completed by his successor Hadrian, is being restored by German archaeologists. Building such temples had financial and political benefits, attracting patronage from emperors and fostering closer ties with Rome. To the south of the acropolis, in the main town, was a Serapeum – a temple to the Egyptian god Serapis, which later became the site of a Christian church known as the 'Red Basilica'. The Christian community at Pergamum was one of the Seven Churches of Asia to which the Book of Revelation was addressed.

The most famous religious building in Pergamum, however, is no longer there, having been removed wholesale by German archaeologists between 1879 and 1904. This is the Altar of Zeus, also known as the Pergamon Altar, now housed in the Pergamon Museum in Berlin. Erected by Eumenes II after victorious campaigns against the Galatians, it ostensibly commemorated his father's famous defeat of the same foes, although it also encoded a wider message about Pergamum's status in the Greek world. It was a stepped square podium mounted to a terrace with a central altar surrounded by a horseshoe-shaped colonnade, upon which was mounted a huge 113-metre (371-feet) long frieze of the Gigantomachy or war between the Olympian gods and the Titans, along with other mythological scenes. After the sculptures of Phidias from the Parthenon, this frieze is considered to be the highest achievement of Classical Greek sculpture (Pergamum was famous for its sculpture). In the Gigantomachy, the Olympians triumph over the forces of chaos (the Titans), bringing order and harmony to the world. The Pergamenes intended this to symbolize their role as the true protectors of the Greek world order, a mantle they had assumed from the now declining Athens. The altar also included a frieze of the story of Telephos, mythical founder of Pergamum. This was an attempt to assert the prehistoric divine antecedents of the city and its rulers in the face of the wider Greek view that they were parvenus.

The Library

Pergamum's primacy attracted many scholars, poets, philosophers and scientists, and the Attalids themselves were keen collectors of scrolls and books. The centre of this intellectual activity was the Library of Pergamum,

The Trajaneum – a temple to the cult of the emperor Trajan – on the Pergamese Acropolis. This temple is currently being restored by German archaeologists.

A view along the Sacred Way that led from the main city to the Asklepieion, looking from the latter towards the former, with the Acropolis visible on the hilltop in the distance.

second only to its fierce rival the Library of Alexandria. Ancient writers claimed that it housed 200,000 scrolls, although this is probably a substantial exaggeration, with the existing ruins suggesting a more modest 17,000. The library included reading rooms and document storage shelves, and was said to have a built-in air conditioning system of vents to help keep the scrolls and books dry. Supposedly it met its demise when Mark Anthony had

which could be folded repeatedly to make books) was invented at Pergamum when Ptolemy of Egypt decreed that papyrus would no longer be exported, and that this is how parchment got its name (by derivation from the city's name). In practice, parchment had long been in use before Ptolemy, but it is possible that Egyptian shortages forced the Pergamenes to start using parchment or refine their production of it.

The Asklepieion

A few kilometres to the south of the main city was the Asklepieion, a sort of spa-hospital complex, including a temple to Asklepios – god of healing, baths, apartments, a theatre, treatment rooms, a library and a dream incubation facility (see box above). Developed to its fullest extent under the Romans, especially Hadrian, the Asklepieion was accounted one of the wonders of the Roman world, attracting patients and scholars from all over, including famous names such as Aristides and Galen (the 2nd-century CE Pergamene physician whose works formed the basis of Western medicine for the next 1,600 years). Therapies on offer included hot and cold baths, mud treatments, prayer and all the benefits of Greco-Roman medicine.

the entire collection removed and given as a wedding gift to Cleopatra, to replenish the Library of Alexandria.

Another popular legend attached to the Library of Pergamum derives from Pliny, who claimed that parchment (also referred to as vellum – paper made from treated, scraped and stretched animal hides,

EPHESUS

LOCATION: AEGEAN COAST OF TURKEY

DATE OF CONSTRUCTION: 10TH CENTURY BCE

ABANDONED: c 15TH CENTURY CE

BUILT BY: GREEK COLONISTS

KEY FEATURES: ARTEMISION; ODEON; LIBRARY OF CELSUS; GREAT THEATRE; DOUBLE CHURCH OF THE VIRGIN AND ST JOHN; BATHS OF CONSTANTINE; STATUES OF THE AMAZONS

Each year tens of thousands of tourists tramp around a collection of dusty ruins many miles inland from the sea, gawping at cracked flagstone paving, the occasional row of low, crumbled shop fronts and the reconstructed façade of an ancient library, before reaching a marshy rectangular depression. Here a single column and a few scattered blocks of stone are all that remain of what was once the largest building in the ancient Greek world and the heart of one of the greatest cities of the ancient world.

Eighteen hundred years ago a visitor would have been greeted with a very different prospect, for this was Ephesus, the greatest city in Asia Minor, the richest port in the Roman Empire and the site of the Temple of Artemis, a cult site of extreme antiquity and one of the Seven Wonders of the Ancient World. The visitor's eye would have delighted at the great mass of public buildings in white marble; the busy docks, lapped by the waters of the Aegean and thronged with the trade of many nations; the mule trains and wagons carrying goods and people back and forth from the Anatolian hinterland; the barges and river boats on the River Cayster; the lush, fertile farmland on the plain all about and above all, the colossal temple with its crowds of priests, astrologers, mountebanks, disputatious Christians, entertainers, hawkers, craftsmen and pilgrims, hailing from distant lands from Persia to Britain.

City of the Amazons

The city had been founded by Athenian and Ionian Greek colonists in around the 10th century BCE on the site of an older Hittite settlement called Apasa. Low hills surrounded by fertile though marshy plains commanded the course of the River Cayster or Kaystros (Küçük Menderes in modern-day Turkish) where it flowed into the Aegean, and here the Greeks built their city, subsuming a pre-existing cult site sacred to the local goddess Cybele, whom the newcomers associated with Artemis, and who would later incorporate many aspects of fertility and virgin-huntress goddesses from all over the ancient world. Later the Greeks claimed mythical origins for the city, attributing its founding to the Amazons, and after them to the 11th-century BCE Athenian prince, Androclus.

The colony prospered, producing some of the first coins ever minted, c 700 BCE, but in the 7th century BCE was sacked by rampaging Cimmerians who burned down the Artemision (Temple of Artemis). Later it fell into Lydian hands when it was besieged by Croesus. He used his legendary wealth to help rebuild the Artemision. When Cyrus of Persia conquered Lydia in 547 BCE, Ephesus fell under Persian dominion, but the Persian emperors, out of respect for the temple, left it unmolested. In 334 BCE the city welcomed Alexander the Great, who re-established its democratic govern-

The Great Theatre at Ephesus, site of gladiatorial combats and the scene of a huge riot triggered by the anti-pagan preaching of Paul of Tarsus.

ment, and it then passed into the control of his general Lysimachus, who relocated many of the inhabitants from the low-lying marshy plains to the hills and enclosed the city with a defensive wall.

Roman and Byzantine Ephesus

Lysimachus was defeated by the Seleucids, but they in turn gave way to the Romans who handed the city over to Pergamum (see page 46), although in 133 BCE it returned to Roman control. Under the Romans Ephesus vied with Pergamum for the status of chief city of Asia, eventually becoming the capital of the province of Asia, while its mercantile activities made it for a while the richest port in the empire. Roman control of Ephesus continued unbroken except for the uprising of Mithridates VI of Pontus in 88 BCE. Corrupt Roman tax farmers and speculators had aroused the ire of the Asians and Mithridates incited the Asian cities to rise up against their Roman overlords and massacre every Latin in Asia. Even those who tried to claim sanctuary at the Artemision (see below) were slaughtered. Estimates of the death toll range from 80–150,000. When the Roman general Sulla defeated Mithridates and crushed the uprising, Ephesus escaped with a heavy fine.

From the 1st century CE Ephesus flourished, growing to around 225,000 inhabitants (some authorities claim it was much larger, with up to 500,000 inhabitants, which would probably have made it the largest city in the world at the time). Many impressive buildings were constructed and the city was provided with some of the most extensive aqueducts and other hydrological infrastructure of the ancient world. The Artemision, too, continued to flourish, although it became a major focus of discontent for the growing Christian community, including St Paul, who famously triggered a riot when his preaching angered idol-makers at the temple, prompting them to gather a huge mob at the city's gigantic theatre (site of contests between gladiators, some of whom were buried at a recently discovered graveyard in the city). Ephesus was to become one of the most important dioceses of the nascent Church, with cult sites such as the tomb of St John the Apostle and the last resting place of the Virgin Mary. Major church councils were held there, but eventually it lost influence and power to Constantinople.

Under the Byzantines the city declined, its population reduced by malaria from the surrounding marshes and its fabric degraded by a series of assaults and sackings: by the Arabs in 655 and 717, the Iconoclasts in the 8th and 9th centuries, the Seljuk Turks in 1090 and the early 14th century, Catalonian mercenaries in the pay of Byzantium, then the Turks again, Tamerlane in 1403 and a series of feuding emirs throughout the rest of the 15th century. In 1439 Mark of Ephesus visited Florence for a council bringing together the Eastern and Western Churches, and although he treated the Latins with great disdain and haughtiness, he was, in the words of the *Catholic Encyclopaedia*, merely 'the pastor of a

The partially restored façade of the Library of Celsus, the most impressive ruin in Ephesus. The library held 12,000 scrolls.

A mosaic of a duck – part of a larger mosaic from one of the main streets of Ephesus, and symbolic of the extraordinary wealth of a city that could pave its streets with expensive art.

lies nearby, this library held 12,000 scrolls. Cunning architecture, involving a convex lower tier, makes the façade seem bigger than it really is.

From the centre of town the Sacred Way, also known as the Marble Street, leads to the Great Theatre, which has seating for 25,000. A broad road known as Arcadiane ran from here to the port, passing on the right the great Baths of Constantine, so large that visitors would sometimes mistake them for the Artemision. In the northwest of the ancient city lay the Double Church of the Virgin and St John, where the early church councils were held.

miserable village'. By this time the city's ancient harbour had long-since silted up and it now lies some 5 kilometres (3 miles) inland.

Main Buildings of Ephesus

Excavations by mainly British and Austrian archaeologists have revealed some of the splendour of ancient Ephesus. Paved streets (some paved with marble, others with mosaics) and colonnades lead to some impressive surviving or rebuilt structures. The *odeon* was a roofed theatre used for musical performances, poetry readings and prize-giving; it had seating for 2,200 people. Next to it was the *agora* or public square, with large halls, columns, porticoes and shops. Curetes Street runs west from here to the town centre, close to which is the most impressive extant façade in Ephesus – the Library of Celsus. Built to honour the recently deceased proconsul of Asia, T. Julius Celsus, whose tomb

The Artemision

The ancient Greek writer Antipater of Thessalonica wrote that although he had seen the Hanging Gardens of Babylon, the Colossus of Rhodes, the Mausoleum and the Pyramids, none compared to the glories of the Artemision, 'when I saw the house of Artemis that mounted to the clouds, those other marvels lost their brilliancy, and I said, "Lo, apart from Olympus, the Sun never looked on aught so grand."'

The colossal temple, situated a little way off from the main city, was rebuilt several times. It was relatively small (originally just an altar on a platform of green schist) until Croesus paid for a huge Ionic temple, built entirely of marble and incorporating 127 columns. This incarnation of the temple was 116 metres (380½ feet) long and 55 metres (180½ feet) wide, covering an area of about 7,430 square metres (79,975 square feet). According to Pliny it was built on marshy ground to help protect it from earthquakes and took 120 years to complete, finally being consecrated sometime between 430 and 420 BCE. Among the many treasures with which it was endowed were a series of bronze statues of Amazons created for a competition by the leading sculptors of the day, including Phidias who made the famous chryselephantine statues of Zeus and Athena Parthenos.

According to the ancient scribes, this version of the temple was destroyed in 356 BCE (on the same night as the birth of Alexander the Great), when a man named Herostratus set fire to the wooden frame of the roof, hoping to win eternal renown (or at least infamy) for his evil deed. It was soon rebuilt, this time with columns 18 metres (59 feet) high and continued to attract crowds of pilgrims, priests and hangers-on, generating considerable industry and income for the city. A coin from the reign of Claudius (c 50 CE) shows the temple pediment with three windows or openings, which were probably used to display either the famous bronze Amazons or images of the goddess herself. But the version of Artemis worshipped at Ephesus was very different from those of Athens or the Roman Diana. The Ephesian Artemis-Cybele combined prehistoric traditions with Persian and other influences, to produce a complex iconography featuring a woman with many breasts (that may actually have symbolized eggs, bees or the testicles of sacrificial bulls) and other symbols of fecundity and natural bounty.

An important feature of the temple was the right to asylum that applied within its sacred bounds, which meant

Public toilets, probably from Roman Ephesus, thoughtfully designed for use while seated or standing. Romans cleaned their bottoms with sponges on sticks, which were rinsed in buckets but shared by all comers.

that criminals, fugitives and those in fear of their lives could not be harmed or arrested once they passed within its precincts. Under Mark Anthony the boundaries of asylum were extended to include parts of the city proper, which resulted in that quarter degenerating into a den of vice. The inviolate nature of the sacred precincts also made the Artemision a safe place to store money, and great quantities of treasure were banked here for safekeeping.

Although it was sacked and burned by the Goths in 262 CE, it was at least partially restored and continued to be a major religious centre until the Edict of Theodosius forced the closing of the pagan temples, and its stones were quarried for the construction of a nearby cathedral. Some were even burnt for lime. By the time of the Ottoman conquest the site was buried under 1 metre (3¼ feet) of silt, and today a single forlorn pillar marks the spot where this ancient wonder once stood.

PALMYRA

LOCATION: CENTRAL SYRIA

DATE OF CONSTRUCTION: *c* 330 BCE

ABANDONED: *c* 6TH CENTURY CE

BUILT BY: PALMYRENES

KEY FEATURES: TARIFF OF PALMYRA; TEMPLE OF BEL; PROPYLEA; THEATRE; COLUMNS; DIOCLETIAN BATHS; HYBRID CULTURAL INFLUENCES

The ruins of ancient Palmyra are among the world's most impressive remnants of lost cities. Graceful columns of rose-hued stone soar into the desert sky along colonnaded streets, recalling the city's former elegance and beauty. Yet appearances might be regarded as deceptive, for the animating impulses of Palmyra were trade and money rather than art or culture, and for a brief period it was the trading centre of the Mediterranean-Oriental world.

Palmyra is the Greek name for the city of Tadmor, probably derived from the Semitic word for 'palm tree'. Known as the Bride of the Desert, Palmyra was an oasis city in the centre of Syria, 215 kilometres (133½ miles) northeast of Damascus. It lay on the border between the semi-arid Badiya, or Syrian steppe, and the wide expanse of desert that separates it from the upper reaches of the Euphrates. The city's form and culture were a classic marriage of East and West, with Hellenistic and Roman influences melded to Arabic, Egyptian, Mesopotamian and Persian ones. Famous as the home of the legendary Queen Zenobia, it is now also renowned as one of the most beautiful ruins in the world. What you can see today is effectively a snapshot of a Roman city frozen at the height of the empire's glory, a city undone by hubris and the vengeance of Rome.

Merchant City

Biblical tradition attributes the founding of Tadmor to Solomon (*c* 1000 BCE), but it is extremely unlikely that Hebrew kings ever ruled this region, while Assyrian inscriptions on tablets found at the ancient city of Mari on the Euphrates dating back to *c* 1800 BCE, show that a settlement had existed there since the Bronze Age. Hot springs provided a constant supply of water (as well as a faint smell of sulphur characteristic of the city), attracting caravans crossing the arid wastes between the Euphrates – which gave access to the trade of Persia, the Gulf of Arabia, India and China and the Silk Road – and Damascus and points west. But at this point it may have been little more than a tent city.

According to some sources, Alexander the Great and his successors, the Seleucids, founded a more permanent city and gave it a Hellenistic constitution, but even in 41 BCE, when Mark Anthony led a cavalry raid across the desert to plunder its riches, Palmyra's inhabitants were sufficiently mobile to have vacated the city along with all their moveable goods (having received advanced warning of his attack). It was officially absorbed into the Roman province of Syria in 17 CE, and Roman influence was to make the city one of the richest in the Near East.

The heyday of Palmyra came in the 2nd century CE when Roman road building caused a major shift in the

trade routes, and an increasing quantity of merchandise that had previously flowed through Petra (see page 34) now travelled via Palmyra. The city's prosperity was cemented when the Roman emperor Hadrian visited in 129 CE, granting Palmyra 'free city' status, with attendant financial and regulatory benefits, after which it became known as Hadriana Palmyra. Later the city was made capital of the Roman province of Syria Phoenice. At its peak, there were some 30,000 inhabitants.

In 217 CE the city received a further boost from the part-Syrian emperor Caracalla, who awarded it official 'colony' status, which exempted it from imperial taxes. Palmyra was now at the height of its prosperity. Grand civic buildings in the Roman style were complemented by great temples, rich merchant's mansions and

Gracious colonnades of ancient Palmyra, with the Arab fort of Qalaat ibn Ma'an in the background. The set of four quadruple pillars in the centre is the remains of the Tetrapylon, which marked the intersection of two colonnaded streets.

elaborate tombs. Pillars and inscriptions have preserved important information about this era, illustrating how trade was the lifeblood of the city.

The famous Tariff of Palmyra is an inscription from around 137 CE, setting out financial and tax laws, detailing the commodities that passed through Palmyra and the levels of taxes and duties levied on them. As well as taxes on goods from ivory and silk to precious gems and spices, the tariff also records levies on other commodities and commercial activities from water to prostitution. The city's financial authority – known as the 'treasurers' – were as or more important than its civic governance and were actively involved in helping to set up and even fund trade ventures. Large camel trains, for instance, which might be beyond the means of an individual merchant or even a group of merchants, would be underwritten by the city itself. The city's mercantile reach extended as far as the Mediterranean and the Indian Ocean, where ships owned by Palmyrenes plied the waters off Italy and controlled the silk trade from the Far East.

Queen Zenobia, Empress of all Asia
Although Palmyra was now an official Roman colony it remained very much on the borders of the empire, a useful buffer between Rome and its eastern rivals, the Parthians. When the Romans were succeeded as masters of Persia and Mesopotamia by the Sassanids in the 3rd century CE, however, trouble began to brew. In 227 CE the Sassanids closed their end of the caravan routes, dealing a heavy blow to Palmyran trade. Over the next few decades Rome and the Sassanids clashed repeatedly, culminating in 259 CE with the capture of the Roman emperor Valerian and the loss of significant territory.

At this time the ruler of Palmyra was a local prince, Septimus Odaenathus, whom the Romans had appointed governor of Syria Phoenice; it was to him that Rome turned to avenge their losses. Vigorous campaigning saw him regain much of the lost territory and in 260 CE he was recognized by Rome as Corrector Totius Orientis – Governor of all the East. But Odaenathus had greater ambitions. He proclaimed himself king and later emperor, but in 267 CE he was assassinated in mysterious circumstances and his wife, Queen Zenobia, took over the regency on behalf of their infant son.

The impressive entrance to the amphitheatre. Note the Roman (semi-circular) arches resting on Corinthian capitals.

Zenobia proved to be one of the most remarkable women in history. Of mixed Greek-Arab descent she was renowned for her beauty and intelligence. Well educated and fluent in several languages, she attracted philosophers, artists and poets to her court, but was also renowned as a superb horsewoman and a capable general. Under her rule, Palmyra briefly flowered into an empire as she took advantage of Roman weakness to conquer the Levant, Egypt and much of Asia Minor. But her career as empress was short-lived. Emperor Aurelian marshalled his legions, reconquered the lost territories and besieged Zenobia at Palmyra in 272 CE. Eventually she was captured and taken as a prisoner to be paraded through the streets of Rome in golden chains, along with her son. Accounts of her end are varied – in some versions she committed suicide or was beheaded, while in others Diocletian gave her a villa in Tivoli and she married a senator and became a popular fixture of Roman society.

The Romans never forgave Palmyra, especially after the city again rebelled in 273 CE, and it was looted and razed. Later the emperor Diocletian made it a garrison town, but it never recovered its glory. Under the Byzantines it was an important religious centre but the trade routes had once again shifted and it was not until the time of Saladin, in the 12th century, that the city enjoyed a brief rebirth before shrinking again to an obscure village that was 'rediscovered' by British travellers in 1751. Reports and engravings of the beautiful ruins sparked a Palmyrene craze in Europe and the US, and design features from ancient Palmyra were all the rage. For instance, a design of an eagle from the ceiling of the Temple of Bel (see below) was incorporated into the Seal of the United States.

The Temple of Bel, Palmyra's main temple, which displays a mixture of architectural influences, including Greek, Roman and Semitic, reflecting the diverse ethnic and cultural mix of the city.

East Meets West

Palmyra was a strikingly mixed city, reflecting the various influences that created it. It had a Greek constitution, Seleucid dating, Macedonian calendar, Semitic alphabet and Aramaic as its everyday language, although Greek and Latin were also in use and inscriptions were often in two or three languages. Leading citizens took local (Semitic) and Roman names, e.g. Malé Agrippa, the wealthy merchant who paid for the lavish celebrations that marked the visit of Hadrian in 129 CE or Wahballat Athenodoros, the son of Odaenathus and Zenobia.

This mixed heritage was reflected in the physical fabric of the city. Colonnaded streets, baths, a theatre and an *agora* speak clearly to the Greco-Roman influence, as do the Classical Greek floorplans of the merchants' mansions excavated by archaeologists, complete with beautiful mosaics. The city's main temple, dedicated to the Babylonian god Bel, featured Greek columns around the *cella* (the inner chamber) and imitative Graeco-Roman pediments, but the overall layout of the *temenos*, or sacred district, was based on Semitic models (like the Temple of Solomon). Also Semitic was the custom of accessing the temple's roof from the *cella*, and using it as the stage of processions and sacrifices.

Visitors today can still see many remains. The theatre has been partially restored and is probably the highlight, with a grand backdrop to the main stage, designed to resemble the façade of a palace. Originally it was three storeys high. Many columns still stand along the main colonnaded street, with richly decorated monumental archways and the remains of the Temple of Neb (the Babylonian god of writing and wisdom). The street leads towards the Diocletian Baths (built between 293 and 303 CE, when the city was mainly a garrison town), notable for four pink sandstone columns probably brought all the way from Egypt. It may originally have been intended as a palace, but was requisitioned for its new role when the military moved in.

EUROPE

From Bronze Age Knossos to doomed Pompeii, the cities in this chapter span 1,500 years of history, yet there is a clear connection and sense of continuity running through their four stories, which chart the development of the Classical world in Europe from its earliest times to the threshold of its greatest empire. Until the late 19th century it had been believed that European civilization started with the ancient Greeks in around 800 BCE, but Schliemann's excavations at Mycenae, which appeared to reveal a High Bronze Age culture corresponding to the Achaeans of Homer (see page 40), with their great king Agamemnon and their heroes such as Achilles and Ajax, pushed this date back to at least 1500 BCE. Schliemann's discoveries inspired the excavation of Knossos, which revealed an even older civilization – the Minoans: the first European civilization.

A cultural thread runs from this early European civilization at Knossos through the Mycenaeans to the Greeks and eventually from them to the Romans, and this thread links all four cities in this chapter. Akrotiri, on modern-day Santorini (but originally on a much larger island that was largely destroyed when the volcano of Thera erupted in a colossal explosion c 1625 BCE), was a town of the Cycladic culture with close ties to the dominant Minoan culture on Crete, but which also traded with Mycenae on mainland Greece. Entremont, in southern France (then Gaul), was a settlement on the fringes of the Greco-Roman world, built by Celto-Ligurians, but inspired by and modelled on nearby Greek colonies, and later closely involved with the expanding empire of Rome. Pompeii was a thriving city of late Republican Rome (although originally Latin rather than Roman) and at one time may well have been the base for merchants and artisans who traded with Entremont. Through the stories of these four cities we can follow the development and spread of European civilization.

Frescoes in the Villa of Mysteries in Pompeii. This unique series of megalographia, or lifesize murals, is believed by some to show stages of the initiation rites of the Dionysian Mysteries.

AKROTIRI

LOCATION: SANTORINI, GREECE
DATE OF CONSTRUCTION: c 2000 BCE
ABANDONED: 1625 OR 1545 BCE
BUILT BY: CYCLADIC CULTURE
KEY FEATURES: FRESCOES; TWO-STOREY HOUSES; LUSTRAL BASINS

Gracious houses decorated with delightful frescoes and finely carved furniture crowd together around a harbour under a bright blue Mediterranean sky. The wharves are busy with sailors and dockhands buzzing to and fro, overseen by prosperous merchants. But far beneath them a huge mass of magma seethes and roils, threatening to unleash a cataclysm. Ancient Akrotiri was a picture of bourgeois bliss, but this middle-class paradise was built on a volcano that was about to erupt in the most enormous explosion ever witnessed by civilization.

Around 1625 BCE (or possibly 1545 BCE – there is fierce dispute over the exact dating) the volcanic island of Thera, one of the Cyclades islands between mainland Greece and Crete, exploded in an eruption that measured 7 on the Volcanic Explosivity Index – 100 times more powerful than the eruption of Mt St Helens in 1980. The tsunamis generated by the eruption would have been up to 150 metres (492 feet) high according to some estimates. Four times as much material was ejected into the atmosphere as during the famous explosion at Krakatau in 1883 and a blanket of ash and rock up to 50 metres (164 feet) thick settled on the remnants of the island (today the shattered island is an archipelago known as Santorini). Buried beneath this volcanic fallout was the ancient seaport at modern Akrotiri, which lay hidden for three and half millennia

until in 1967 renowned Greek archaeologist Spyridon Marinatos began excavations.

What he revealed, and subsequent excavations continue to investigate, was a Cycladic version of Pompeii (see page 72), but with important differences from the Roman town. Whereas the unfortunate Latins were caught unawares and suffered grisly deaths, the inhabitants of Akrotiri seem to have managed to evacuate the town, taking all their portable valuables with them. No uninterred human remains have been found nor have any precious objects, with one exception, an intriguing golden ibex figurine that was hidden beneath a floor – perhaps simply forgotten or perhaps buried for ritual reasons, like figurines found in Neolithic Çatalhöyük (see page 16).

A detail of one of the most famous frescoes in Akrotiri, which shows two boys returning from a fishing expedition, loaded with the fish they have caught. This fresco is found in the parlour of a building known as the West House, believed to have belonged to a naval commander. One expert on the site has suggested that the boys are his sons; others have argued that the boys are shown having successfully completed a rite of passage, or are bringing offerings to a goddess. The fish that the boy is carrying have been identified as dolphinfish.

Cosmopolitan Harbour Town

When the ancient Akrotirians fled they left behind a sophisticated urban development, with spacious multi-storey houses of high-quality masonry equipped with advanced plumbing and sewers, and adorned with vivid and graceful art as fine as any Mediterranean civilization has ever produced. The first settlements on this site date back as far as the Neolithic Era, to before the 4th millennium BCE, but the town reached its height in the Minoan Era (2000–c 1500 BCE), by which time it had grown into one of the major Bronze Age ports in the eastern Mediterranean. The flourishing palace culture of the Minoans in Crete carried on extensive trade with other Bronze Age superpowers of Egypt, Asia Minor and the Levant, while on the Greek mainland the Mycenaean civilization was gathering strength. Goods and people passed back and forth across the Aegean and Akrotiri was at the centre of this trade – objects have been found there from Crete, Egypt, Anatolia, Cyprus, Syria and the Greek mainland and islands.

The wealth garnered by this trade helped turn Akrotiri into a prosperous town that covered around 20 hectares (49½ acres) and had a population of several thousand. Excavations have shown that although the streets were relatively narrow (probably too narrow for wheeled carts, but wide enough for pack animals), the houses were quite grand. Mostly built of rubble masonry between timber frames, but

Pottery excavated at Akrotiri. When the inhabitants fled, they took their most valuable possessions but left behind many everyday objects such as jars and bowls, providing a treasure trove for the archaeologist. Analysis of the clay reveals that the majority of pottery was made on Thera, but significant quantities were imported from Crete. Similarly, the decorative motifs, even when domestically produced, demonstrate many foreign – primarily Minoan – influences.

with some sophisticated dressed-stone block masonry in places (especially on public buildings), many of them were two or even three storeys high. Inside, the lower rooms were probably utilitarian, with kitchen amenities such as mill installations for grinding corn, pestles and mortars for food preparation and large sunken jars for storing supplies. The upper rooms, however, where the owners lived and socialized, were large and airy with big windows. The interiors were plastered and often decorated with the beautiful frescoes that are Akrotiri's most famous legacy.

Some houses had toilets, with wooden benches with openings to clay pipes that connected to the municipal sewers – narrow stone-lined trenches that ran beneath the streets. In some places twin sets of pipes bringing water into houses suggest that the Akrotirians had hot and cold running water – the former perhaps supplied by hot springs on the volcanic island. Some houses even had separate bathrooms, with walls plastered halfway up to guard against splashing, just like our modern bathrooms. These rooms were painted yellow and may have been equipped with clay bathtubs and bronze vessels for bringing water, such as have been found in one of the settlement's houses. One of the public buildings has a lustral basin – a sunken stone-lined pool probably used for ritual washing. Such sophisticated plumbing is remarkable for an ancient town.

A MINOAN COLONY?

Akrotiri is often described as a Minoan colony or the most famous Minoan site outside Crete. It undoubtedly had strong links with the palace-based culture of the Minoans, as shown by cultural correspondences such as similarities between its frescoes and those found in Crete (for instance, a recent find from Xeste 4 is of fragments of fresco possibly showing bull-leaping, a signature Minoan motif which had been thought absent from Theran art), with other features such as the lustral basin, and by its material culture in terms of pottery and other artefacts. But it is thought likely that it was more representative of the ancient Cycladic culture that had flourished on the Cyclades since *c* 3000 BCE and that its inhabitants were indigenous, but inevitably influenced by the dominant culture to the south; they probably also absorbed influences from Egypt and other important Bronze Age civilizations.

The End of Akrotiri

Marinatos's excavation revealed evidence that Akrotiri had suffered major earthquake damage before it was buried in ash from the eruption of Thera. He theorized that it was this earthquake that had given the inhabitants sufficient warning to evacuate. In practice, the picture is slightly more complex. The careful piling of rubble and the presence of great stone 'demolition' balls probably similar to modern wrecking balls (although it has been suggested that these are merely natural volcanic ejecta), indicates that after an initial earthquake there was a planned programme of demolition to clear unsafe houses and prepare for reconstruction. It is also clear that this programme of reconstruction was well under-way when the evacuation came – and possibly had been for years. Evidently there was sufficient warning – perhaps from small tremors or perhaps from an initial, minor eruption and ash-fall – that a major eruption was on the way, for this rebuilding was abruptly halted. In the building known as the West House, where plastering and painting was apparently still in progress and was left half-finished, abandoned vessels of plaster and paint have been found.

When the eruption came a deep layer of pumice and ash covered the island so thickly that it was uninhabitable for centuries. Exactly what became of the Akrotirians is impossible to know, but the consequences of the eruption may have been far-reaching. Marinatos was led to begin his excavations at Akrotiri by his theory that the eruption triggered the collapse of Minoan civilization, but in practice the dates do not match up. The palace culture probably survived for another century after Thera exploded, but there is little doubt that the volcano had an impact. While the prevailing winds meant that most of Crete was not hit by the fallout, the vast tsunami generated by the eruption must have pulverized the Minoan fleet and all the towns along its northern seaboard. Many Atlantologists even claim that the destruction of Thera was the basis for the legend of Atlantis (although in practice Atlantis was probably purely an invention of Plato's, and not based on a real place).

The Frescoes

The most striking survivors of the eruption are the many frescoes that decorate the inside of every building in Akrotiri. Only a few of the rooms in each house are decorated and the subjects dealt with vary widely. For instance, in the building known as Xeste 3 (from the Greek *xeste*, meaning 'dressed masonry', such as is seen on this building, probably indicating that it was a public building and thus somewhat grander than the private houses), which features a lustral basin, the frescoes appear to show parts of a procession or religious ritual/festival. On the upper floor young women are shown gathering crocuses and bringing them to a central female figure, perhaps a goddess, who is flanked by worshipping animals – a griffin and a monkey. On the ground floor a fresco on one wall shows a girl carrying a necklace, a girl who has hurt her foot, which is bleeding, and a girl walking in one direction but

facing in the other. One wall is dominated by a fresco of a closed door crowned with horns dripping with blood.

By contrast the private houses show more secular scenes. The building known as the West House, for instance, features a famous fresco of two young fishermen, bearing skeins of fish, while another room shows a fleet of ships crossing the sea and putting in at port, while on another wall of the same room two ships disgorge warriors in boar's-tusk helmets. Another room in the house is decorated with a frieze of a repeated motif of the stern cabin of a ship.

Interpreting these frescoes at a distance of 3,500 years is hard, but ancient historian Fritz Schachermeyr takes a personal slant. He identifies the house with the fleet frescoes as belonging to the commander of such a fleet – the main fresco is an account of one of his journeys and the port shown is Akrotiri itself. Meanwhile, he has decorated his own bedroom with cabins because of their personal significance, while the two fishing youths in the parlour are his sons.

Schachermeyr also has an influential theory about Akrotiri as a whole. The absence of any palace buildings indicates that there was no ruling family. Rather, the nature of the houses (their size and quality and the expensive fittings and decorations) suggests that there were several rich families, possibly patricians, and the heterogeneous forms taken by the frescoes underline the way that taste and style were not defined by a central authority, but created on an individual basis. All this, he argues, points to Akrotiri being a maritime republic of the type seen throughout history, from Athens and Carthage, Genoa and Venice, to Hamburg and Bremen, Amsterdam and London. In such cities a prosperous merchant class was independent and liberal in governance and thought, and its society prospered as a result. Could Akrotiri have been the first such liberal maritime republic? An engagingly sophisticated and modern society until it was cut off in its prime by an unstoppable cataclysm?

POMPEII

LOCATION: BAY OF NAPLES, ITALY

DATE OF CONSTRUCTION: 6TH CENTURY BCE

ABANDONED: 79 CE

BUILT BY: ETRUSCANS? ROMANS

KEY FEATURES: PRESERVED STREETS AND BUILDINGS; HOUSE OF THE FAUN; HOUSE OF THE VETTII; VILLA OF THE MYSTERIES; THERMOPOLIA; BROTHEL; GRAFFITI; MOSAICS AND MURALS; VOIDS IN FORM OF INCINERATED PEOPLE

Arguably the most important archaeological site in the world, Pompeii is also one of the largest, in terms of coherent, contiguous ruins. But for recent closures to help conserve the fragile site, a modern visitor would be able to explore almost exactly the same geography as his ancient counterpart – an entire city, from the grandest public buildings to the meanest back-alley hovel, preserved to an unprecedented extent by fallout from the eruption of Vesuvius in 79 CE.

Pompeii is a ruined town on the lower slopes of Mount Vesuvius on the Bay of Naples. In its heyday as many as 20,000 people lived there and the town was prosperous thanks to the rich, fertile volcanic soils of the region, local industry, maritime trade coming into Italy via the nearby ports (in ancient times it was much closer to the sea than it is now) and the popularity of the Bay of Naples area as a fashionable resort and leisure destination for Roman senators, noblemen and wealthy businessmen.

The oldest settlement on the site dates back to the Iron Age, in the 8th century BCE, although nearby sites date back as far as the Bronze Age, and suffered a similar fate to Pompeii itself – caught unawares by the previous eruption of Vesuvius, some 1,800 years earlier. Pompeii itself was founded in the 6th century BCE, either by a local tribe, the Oscans, or possibly by Greek colonists or the Etruscans. By the 4th century BCE the area

had fallen under the hegemony of Rome, but Pompeii did not become a Roman town until it joined with other towns in the region in an unsuccessful rebellion against Rome, found itself on the losing side and was finally declared a Roman colony in 80 BCE. Many of the buildings visible at Pompeii today, including much of the infrastructure, were built in the Roman period. The reign of Augustus (30 BCE–14 CE) saw particularly intensive building work.

Rough Guide to Pompeii

Excavations have uncovered 44 of the 66 hectares (109 of the 163 acres) occupied by the city. It is roughly oval in shape, with the long axis oriented east-west. A city wall, pierced by seven main gates, encloses the whole. Most visits begin at the Marine Gate in the southwest, which leads almost immediately to the forum, the centre of public life in Pompeii and the site of a bustling market. Around the forum are many of the main public buildings, including the Temples of Apollo and Jupiter, the basilica (where legal business was done), one of the

A fresco (removed from Pompeii and now housed at the National Archaeological Museum in Naples) from the Temple of Isis at Pompeii, showing Isis receiving Io at Canopus. Io (on the left) was a priestess who was turned into a cow at one point, hence the horns.

city's baths, the *macellum* (market/shopping mall) and the local government offices.

Southeast of these is Pompeii's 'leisure complex', a group of buildings including the Samnite Palaestra (a kind of gym), the theatre and the *odeon*, the gladiator's barracks and the Temple of Isis. Although an eastern cult, worship of Isis became extremely popular and this temple was the only one to be fully restored after the earthquake of 62 CE (see below).

Running east from the forum, passing to the north of the leisure zone, is the Via dell'Abbondanza, a long, mostly straight road that runs all the way to the Sarno Gate at the eastern end of the city. Along or just off it can be seen many of the most interesting private or commercial buildings of Pompeii, including a fullery, the brothel, the Stabian Baths and the Thermopolium of Vetutius Placidus. A *thermopolium* was a kind of bar/café, which served hot food to customers who stood at a bar into which were sunk terracotta containers for hot stews, soups, etc. Pompeii's *thermopolia* seem to have done a roaring trade, indicated by the bag of over a thousand coins discovered at one such establishment, believed to be the takings on the day that the eruption struck. The Via dell'Abbondanza leads towards the *palaestra* (exercise courts for wrestling/boxing – a kind of Roman gym) and the amphitheatre. With seating for 20,000 people this is the oldest stone amphitheatre in the world. Gladiatorial games were staged here, but it was closed down for a decade from 59 CE after spectators from Pompeii and the nearby town of Nuceria started a riot. North of the Via dell'Abbondanza are the main parts of the city that have yet to be excavated.

The Via di Mercurio (Mercury Street). The raised curbs and the stepping stones in the middle distance allow carts and horses through while also letting pedestrians cross the street without walking through mud and dung. Mount Vesuvius looms in the background.

Opposite: A bakery at Pompeii, with the runner (top half) of a millstone in the foreground (note the slot where a stave could be inserted so that the stone could be turned) and oven in the background.

Above: The lararium *(shrine of the household gods or Lares) of a thermopolium at Pompeii, including one of the few frescoes left at the site. Most have been removed to Naples.*

In the northwest section of Pompeii are some of the most interesting and important private houses. For instance, the House of the Vettii is one of the most famous in Pompeii. The owners are thought to have been the Vettii brothers, whose signet rings were discovered on the site. They may have been wine merchants and used their riches to create a beautiful and stylish house that would show off their wealth and taste. In particular, they created a large garden that can be seen from the street through the front door; it was decorated with marble and bronze statues, some

of which spouted water into basins. Around the garden is a portico, decorated with elaborate murals.

Diagonally across an intersection from here is the House of the Faun, named for the statue of a 'faun' (actually a satyr) found at the site. The largest private house in Pompeii, it was possibly built in the 2nd century BCE and after the Roman conquest it may well have housed one of the city's new rulers. Its interior was decorated to underscore the wealth and prestige of its occupant, with massive and extremely detailed (and therefore enormously expensive) mosaics, including the famous

A plaster cast of one of the victims of Vesuvius at Pompeii. The cast was made by filling the void left by the disintegrated body of a Pompeian who had been buried in ash and pumice stones.

replica of a Greek painting showing Alexander the Great defeating the Persian king Darius at the Battle of Issus, which is made up of over a million *tesserae* (tiny tiles).

Leaving from the city's north-western gate, the Herculaneum Gate, the visitor passes through a cemetery and then reaches the Villa of the Mysteries, which gets its name from the *megalographia* (lifesize mural) that runs around all four walls of one of the rooms. This unique frieze is believed by many to show various stages of initiation into the rites of the Dionysian Mysteries, one of several religions/personal growth movements that were popular in the ancient world. Only those who were initiated knew the secrets of these Mystery religions and were forbidden to reveal them, so this mural from Pompeii is one of the primary (and only) sources for our knowledge of this important element of Roman life.

The End of Pompeii

In 62 CE a severe earthquake struck the Bay of Naples region, badly damaging many buildings in Pompeii and other towns. Today vulcanologists understand that this was probably an omen of the much worse catastrophe to come, signifying an upwelling of magma through the crust beneath the mountain. With nearly two millennia elapsed since the last eruption, the Romans had no idea what a menace the volcano posed, still less that Vesuvius is of the type of volcano where the longer the period between eruptions, the more serious the next one is likely to be.

Although the 62 CE earthquake caused alarm and fear, and many left the area altogether, there is clear evidence that extensive rebuilding of Pompeii started immediately.

In the years leading up to 79 CE, multiple minor earthquakes, heralding the imminent eruption, struck, causing subsidiary damage to Pompeii. This too was repaired. Pompeii was too prosperous for its citizens to abandon.

Around 1pm in the afternoon on 24 August 79 CE (this is the traditionally attributed date, but cutting edge research at the site has led to the controversial suggestion that the eruption actually took place later that year), after days of tremors, plumes of gas and the ominous failure of springs around the mountain's flanks, Vesuvius erupted. The first phase of the eruption was what vulcanologists call Plinian, in which gas-rich, frothy, highly-pressurized magma from the top of the magma column blasts high into the atmosphere, carrying with it huge chunks of the mountain. A huge mushroom cloud of fire, ash, smoke and rubble reached 30 kilometres (18½ miles) into the air and then began to rain down as ash and light pumice, with the occasional heavy chunk of rock. In this phase of the eruption 2.6 cubic kilometres (½ cubic mile) of rock was blasted skywards at a rate of 150,000 tons a second.

For the people living around Vesuvius this must have been an awesome and terrifying sight, made even more scary when the cloud blotted out the sun and the day turned to blackest night. A steady rain of ash and pumice started to weigh down and then collapse roofs, killing many. Others were killed by falling rocks. But at this stage, although there was panic, there was a relatively low risk of death. Most of the population, generally estimated to be about 12,000 at this point, were able to wade through the ash and light pumice, and flee the town.

The Plinian phase continued for about 18 hours, but around 7pm on the following day the much more lethal Peléan phase began. As the pressure inside the volcano lessened and the heavier, less gassy magma reached the top of the column, the plume of material collapsed to ground level and what had been an airborne cloud turned into a pyroclastic flow – a rolling, ground-hugging avalanche of super-heated gas, smoke and ash, preceded by a shockwave of heat at temperatures up to 800°C (1,472°F). People in its path were either instantly carbonized, or choked and baked within a few seconds. Buried within the layers of ash and loose rock that continued to accrete, their bodies decomposed to leave voids. Ingenious mid-19th century Italian archaeologist Giuseppe Fiorelli would later inject these voids with plaster to create casts, preserving, for our horrid fascination, the forms of people in their death throes, right down to the expressions of terror on their faces.

How many were killed? It is known that virtually the whole population of nearby Herculaneum, which suffered a similar fate, perished in the pyroclastic flow. They had made it as far as the seashore, but tsunamis created by the huge tremors that accompanied the eruption made it impossible to evacuate by ship and the terrible cloud of death caught them sheltering in boat sheds and the seafront arcade. But only around 2,000 bodies have been recovered from Pompeii and the surrounding area, and it is often assumed that most of the inhabitants of Pompeii escaped.

However, contemporary accounts make it clear that for the region as a whole this was a catastrophe of unprecedented scale, suggesting that tens of thousands were lost at minimum. And while it was normal practice to rebuild towns after natural disasters, the Romans never settled at Pompeii again. So perhaps the missing Pompeians did not escape death – it is simply that the fatal cloud overtook them on the roads south from Pompeii and that the huge mass of carbonized bodies lies beneath unexcavated and unexplored countryside.

Pompeii was rediscovered in 1748 and has been progressively excavated ever since. But archaeologists have found evidence that there was extensive salvage and looting of the site in ancient times. As soon as the dust had settled it seems that enterprising Romans returned and dug down to look for valuables. The site is riddled with tunnels and many walls have been bored through.

KNOSSOS

LOCATION: CRETE, GREECE
DATE OF CONSTRUCTION: *c* 1900 BCE
ABANDONED: *c* 1380 BCE
BUILT BY: MINOANS
KEY FEATURES: PALACE; CENTRAL COURT; FRESCOES; PIANO NOBILE; ROYAL APARTMENTS; LUSTRAL BASINS; PLUMBING AND FLUSHING TOILET

Homer's *Odyssey*, generally thought to be a chronicle of the heroes of mighty Bronze Age civilizations, describes Crete as 'a rich and lovely land, densely peopled and boasting ninety cities [including] a great city called Knossos…' Until 1900, few scholars believed that Crete had indeed hosted a Bronze Age civilization, let alone one of the complexity and sophistication suggested by Homer, but a few years of intensive excavation proved not only that the ancient epic had been right, but that Knossos was the centre of perhaps the first civilization in Europe.

Knossos on Crete was the site of the legendary Labyrinth of the Minotaur, constructed by King Minos and penetrated by the hero Theseus with the help of Minos's daughter Ariadne. A mound at a site in northern Crete called Kephala was traditionally identified as the site of Knossos and in the late 19th century, with interest in archaeology mounting and Schliemann making the headlines with his ground-breaking discoveries at Troy (see page 40), attention turned here.

In 1878 the first attempts at systematic excavation were made by a Cretan antiquarian appropriately named Minos Kalokairinos, but his efforts were limited by the Turkish occupation of the island. Schliemann himself was keen to excavate the site, but it was not until 1900, with the expulsion of the Turks, that British historian Arthur Evans was able to acquire the site and start digging in

earnest. Evans had been inspired by Schliemann's discovery of Mycenae, which had pushed back the chronology of civilization in Europe by nearly a thousand years, and had also become intrigued by evidence for another Bronze Age Mediterranean civilization, in the form of clay seals marked with depictions of marine life, which were alien to Mycenae, Egypt or any other known culture, and that seemed to originate from Crete.

In just five years of archaeology, Evans peeled back the layers of the mound at Kephala to reveal a strange and enormous structure, which he immediately identified as the Palace of Minos himself. Within were vivid frescoes, tablets inscribed with an unidentifiable language in a strange script, sophisticated plumbing, well-crafted artefacts and treasures of gold and silver – all the trappings of a new and previously unknown civilization, whom Evans christened Minoans after the legendary king.

Knossos Through the Ages

Over a century of archaeology at Knossos and other, similar sites around Crete, has revealed much about the history of the Minoans. The first settlements at Knossos date back to at least *c* 6000 BCE, with urban civilization developing towards the end of the Early Bronze Age. In the period labelled the Middle Minoan, from about 1900 BCE, Minoan architecture began to take shape and large buildings became a feature of settlements. Eventually these grew to become what are today called palace complexes. At least four major palace complexes have been found on Crete (together with many more lesser and/or suspected ones), with Knossos being the largest.

Archaeologists use the term 'palace complex' because these great structures were obviously much more than simply places of residence for kings or chieftains. They are equipped with extensive storage facilities, workshops, public spaces, cult shrines and ritual spaces, as well as what look like banqueting halls, audience rooms and suites of private chambers. They dominate the settlements of which they are the foci – the palace at Knossos had around 1,300 rooms, while the city around it was relatively small (although estimates of the population vary from as few as 5,000 to as many as 30,000 or even higher) – and it seems likely that they served a variety of functions: government; religious and ceremonial centre; storage and distribution point for food and goods surpluses; industrial and craft workshops and residence for the ruling family/class.

The palaces were the centre of Minoan life for 600 years, with Knossos lasting the longest. The Old Palace or First Palatial period, from 1900 BCE, was cut short by a catastrophic earthquake that brought widespread destruction, but the palaces were rebuilt grander than before and Minoan civilization reached its apogee during the Neopalatial period. But around 1450 BCE fresh disasters struck – probably more earthquakes, but possibly the eruption of Thera (see page 66). In the Postpalatial period most of the palaces except for Knossos were abandoned and

the evidence from the types of pottery, writing and other cultural artefacts at the site suggests that it had been taken over by the Mycenaeans, the warlike and aggressive power that had been rising on the Greek mainland. Perhaps they were responsible for the destruction of the other palaces or perhaps they simply took advantage of a post-cataclysm power vacuum.

Evans' reconstruction of the North Entrance to the Palace of Knossos. Visitors arriving at Knossos by sea would disembark at the nearby port, and enter the palace via this gate.

Around 1380 BCE Knossos was destroyed by fire and abandoned altogether, although what caused the fire is unclear. New settlements sprang up during Classical Greek and Roman times, but in the Middle Ages nearby towns supplanted Knossos and only local traditions connected it to the ancient legends. Thanks to the work of Evans, the excavated and partially reconstructed site has now become Crete's major tourist attraction, but his legacy is double-edged. Although his work captured public imagination and made Minoan studies a major theatre of Mediterranean archaeology, his highly personal and subjective interpretation of the site and his often highly speculative restoration have damaged the archaeological record and confused many historical issues.

The Palace of Knossos

Roughly in the centre of Crete's northern coast (in the suburbs of the modern Cretan capital Heraklion), Knossos was built on a low ridge overlooked by higher hills, in the centre of the broad valley of the River Kairatos, about 8 kilometres (5 miles) from the sea. In Minoan times the area would have been less arid, the hills covered in oak and cypress and productive farmland in the valley. Significantly, the site was obviously not chosen for its defensibility and on the whole the Minoans seem to have had little to fear from civil strife or invasion. Their civilization was stable and peaceful, and through trade and their maritime skill it developed into a mercantile empire that spanned the eastern Mediterranean and forged close links with the Egyptians.

Neopalatial Knossos (i.e. the second palace) was dominated by the palace complex. A small city clustered

The reconstructed Dolphin Fresco from the Queen's Megaron. Recent research suggests that the fresco was originally painted on the floor of the room now known as the Treasury. Themes such as the dolphins show the Minoans' close relationship with the sea.

around the palace, while 'mini-palaces', sometimes called villas, dotted the countryside. The palace itself was vast. The floor area of one of its levels is around 13,000 square metres (139,000 square feet). Given that most of the palace consisted of at least two, and sometimes up to five storeys, the total floor area must have been at least double this. In all there were around 1,300 rooms, with multiple kinked corridors, stairways, anterooms and platforms giving a truly labyrinthine dimension.

All of the Cretan palaces shared the same basic layout and types of feature, but in each case they were arranged in a unique fashion, apparently developing organically with new units added over time. On the other hand, the way that these additional structures were incorporated seamlessly into the infrastructure of the palace suggests that additions were far from haphazard and must have been planned or allowed for.

The basic arrangement is of four wings in a roughly rectangular arrangement around a central court. The court possibly served as a public area – perhaps similar to a Greek *agora* or Roman forum – but may also have simply been a device to ensure maximum access to air and light for rooms in the massive complex. It is clear from the preponderance of features such as lightwells, walls pierced with multiple doorways, multiple windows in upper storeys and open colonnades along corridors, that the Minoans were concerned to ensure the best possible ventilation and lighting for as many rooms as possible.

The other possible use of the central court was as the arena for bull-leaping and other ceremonial sports. Decoration and motifs throughout the palace testify to the importance of the bull as a symbol to the Minoans, most famously in the context of frescoes showing 'bull-leaping' – where young Minoans (both men and women) apparently faced an on-rushing bull and somersaulted between its horns and over its back before landing on their feet behind it. Whether what would have been an incredibly difficult and dangerous sport actually took

place, or was even possible, is unclear. The pictures may be purely fantastical or symbolic. But if it did really happen, the central court would be the obvious arena.

The different wings or blocks around the court seem to have had separate functions. The lower floor of the west wing was mainly devoted to storerooms, known as magazines. These featured stone-lined pits to hold liquids and many large clay jars to hold other goods. Above these was what Evans called the *piano nobile*, by analogy with the *palazzi* of Renaissance Italy. This was an upper storey consisting of 'halls of state', possibly used for audiences, receptions or government business. Also in the west wing were cult rooms – crypt-like rooms with pillars marked with magical or arcane symbols. In particular the double-headed axe blade symbol beloved of the Minoans, and known as a *labrys* in Greek, from which the word labyrinth is derived, features. These symbols may have been intended to help appease the Earth gods and ward off earthquakes.

The east wing of the palace contained suites of rooms that were apparently residential quarters, including areas dubbed by Evans the 'apartments of King Minos', a bathroom with a lustral basin (a sunken bath thought to have had ritual/religious significance) and a toilet room, with arguably the world's earliest flushing toilet. Highly sophisticated plumbing was a major feature of the palace, with aqueducts bringing water and clay pipes carrying away sewage. These pipes were put together using standardized, mass-produced units that tapered along their length to produce a male-female fit giving a waterproof seal – much like modern plumbing components.

Although there were entrances to the palace complex from all sides, the access routes through the surrounding city would have delivered visitors to a ceremonial court in front of the west wing, offering a clear view of the palace. Here the awestruck visitor would be confronted with the vast scale of the complex, while the irregular, broken elevation and skyline of the palace, and the western façade in particular, may have been deliberately intended to confuse the observer and give the impression of a building almost without limits. Together with the maze of corridors, rooms, halls and stairs within, it is not difficult to see where the legend of the Labyrinth arose.

Beyond the palace there are several other important buildings. Linked to the main palace by the Royal Road is the Little Palace, which may have been built to house members of the royal family. To the northwest of the palace are the remains of a shallow stepped bowl, assumed to be a theatre of some sort, possibly for religious ceremonies or bull-leaping. Further to the north, towards the sea, is a building Evans dubbed the 'customs house', because it was on the way in from the harbour. Also in the town is a two-storey building with elaborate plumbing and bathrooms known as the *caravanserai*, (roadside inn) because it was assumed to be a guesthouse.

Minoan Mysteries

The Palace of Knossos seems to encapsulate Minoan civilization. According to archaeologist J. C. McEnroe, Knossos 'is a building that may encompass the breadth and depth of its culture more eloquently than any other single building in the history of European architecture'. Yet despite the evidence of Knossos and the dozens of other sites on Crete, the Minoan civilization remains hedged with mysteries. What were its roots? To what extent was it homegrown? How much inspiration did it draw from the cultures of Egypt, Assyria and the Levant? Where did the palace model come from? Did it evolve from the accretion of smaller elements or was it the product of a single genius, like the Egyptian Imhotep who designed the first pyramids? Was Minoan civilization really a peace-loving, non-militaristic, utopian paradise, as suggested by the general absence of weapons or militaristic art? Or was there a sinister underside of human sacrifice, as suggested by some remains found at Minoan cult sites and by the sinister legend of the Minotaur?

One of the 'magazines' or storage rooms at the Palace of Knossos. These pithoi *(large jars) were filled with grain, olives, dried fish and other staples. Note the handles on the* pithoi, *through which ropes were passed so that they could be more easily handled for transportation.*

Light might be shed on these issues if Minoan language and writing were not also impenetrable mysteries. Clay tablets found at Knossos are inscribed with a script known as Linear A, which seems to encode a language unrelated to any known language and thus impossible to decipher. The graceful, free-spirited art of the Minoans marks them out from other ancient cultures and makes them the object of enduring fascination. It is ironic that we may never solve the many mysteries surrounding them.

ENTREMONT

LOCATION: PROVENCE, FRANCE

DATE OF CONSTRUCTION: *c* 180 BCE

ABANDONED: *c* 90 BCE

BUILT BY: SALYENS

KEY FEATURES: OLD AND NEW TOWN; CITY WALL; HYPOSTYLE HALL; RELIEFS AND IDOLS OF HEADS AND HEROES; OLIVE PRESSES

Traditionally Western European history before the coming of the Romans has been seen as a dark age of savage tribes and primitive villages of rude wattle and daub huts, but a large and sophisticated Gallic settlement in southern France shows that this picture is misconceived.

History only officially begins when it starts to get written down, with the result that pre-literate societies like the pre-Roman Gauls are cast into the darkness of prehistory; relegated, in the traditional historical imagination, to the fringes of the drama – shadowy groups and figures just beyond the reach of the spotlights, lurking offstage, unseen but for brief, bloody incursions into the world of the Greeks and Romans.

As archaeology advances and historical understanding becomes more subtle and informed, many of these groups are moving from prehistory to what is known as protohistory, a discipline in which scant mentions in ancient texts are combined with data from inscriptions, art, artefacts and archaeology to build up a picture of groups, societies, cultures and whole civilizations that were comparable in sophistication and achievement to their better known, more 'advanced' neighbours. Examples include the Scythians and the Celts.

Entremont is a 2nd- to 1st-century BCE settlement of the Celto-Ligurian Salyens (known as the Saluvii by ancient Greco-Roman writers) in Provence in southern France that well illustrates this point. Here, on the fringes of the Greco-Latin world, a large town of regular gridlike streets, massive well-planned fortifications, multiple storey grand public buildings and elaborate religious precincts comparable to the nearby Greek colonies flourished, until besieged and sacked by a Roman army.

Greeks and Gauls

Around 600 BCE Greeks from Phocea founded a colony called Massalia (modern Marseilles) near the mouth of the Rhône, a great river that provided access to much of France and central Western Europe, and via other, closely related river systems, all the way to the British Isles, the Baltic and beyond. All the valuable natural wealth of Europe, from amber and furs to tin and slaves, was available to the Greeks. In return they traded the products of the Mediterranean civilizations – wine, fish products, glass, worked metals, and, above all, quality pottery.

The Greek colony had a significant impact on societies reaching far up into Europe, but especially on those along the Rhône and the Cote d'Azur, the trading routes to and from southern France. And because Greek and Latin writers recorded some of the interactions between the colonists and their neighbours, we know the names of many of these groups. One that particularly stands out was the Salyens, a confederation of tribes of Celts, who had migrated from Central Europe into much of the rest of the continent from around the same time as the foundation of Massalia, and Ligurians, the indigenous peoples of the area.

The Salyens had a fraught relationship with the Greek colony. Although there was considerable trade and peaceful contact, there was also constant tension and occasional outbreaks of violence. In the 4th and 3rd centuries BCE, to protect their trade routes against piracy, the Greeks founded subsidiary colonies along the coast such as Nikaia (Nice) and Antipolis (Antibes), but these too came under threat from land-based forces. The Salyens gained a reputation, in the ancient texts, for extreme barbarity. Their typically Celtic custom of taking heads as trophies made a particular impact on the ancient imagination.

Settlement at Entremont

Entremont is the modern rendering of a medieval name, Intermontes, for a pass from the low valleys of the Arc and Touloubre to a plateau that rose towards the foothills of the Alps. Here, on the southern edge of the plateau, was a natural defensive site controlling the valleys and the passage to the north. What its Celto-Ligurian inhabitants called their settlement is not known, but here they founded what Julius Caesar would later call an *oppidum* – a fortified settlement.

The base of an olive press from Entremont – oil from crushed olives would follow the incised grooves and feed out through the runnel for collection.

The site probably had religious or ritual significance before it was settled, as indicated by *steles* (carved stone posts) from around 500 BCE, that were reused in later buildings, but the first settlement on the site dates back to around 180 BCE. It was small, only about 1 hectare (2½ acres) in area, and was situated at the summit of the plateau. The edges of the settlement

were aligned with the south and west sides of the plateau and it had the shape of a displaced square (i.e. a parallelogram). The northern side of the town, which gave on to the open plateau, was fortified with a 1.36-metre (4½-feet) wide wall that had three towers.

Within this wall 3-metre (10-feet) wide streets were laid out in a regular criss-cross pattern, parallel with the sides of the town, which divided the houses into blocks of around 24 square metres (258 square feet). The streets were not paved, although they were set with stones and fragments of pottery to help stabilize them. Each block of houses was subdivided by walls of stone blocks with mud bricks for their upper courses, into groups of seven simple rooms. Roofs were made of wood frames and wattle and daub. Mud bricks were used to create small structures inside the cell-like houses, such as hearths, but fireplaces were also often built in the street outside the house because of the limited space. One of the blocks was probably devoted to crafts such as metal working, but on the whole the evidence is that the inhabitants of the old town lived at a simple, near-subsistence level, producing little more than they needed for their own survival.

The New Town

Around 150 BCE the town was dramatically enlarged and seems to have taken a step up economically, but there is also evidence of a major shift in the social structure. The new town was much bigger – an area of about 3.5 hectares (8¾ acres) – and had a massive, extensive defensive wall enclosing nearly the whole area of the plateau. This was presumably to prevent attackers from gaining a foothold on level ground. This new wall was 3.5 metres (11½ feet) thick and up to 7 metres (23 feet)

The lower courses of walls were of stone, which has survived to preserve the plan and layout of much of the town. Visible in the foreground are furnaces for metal-working.

high. It had massive protruding towers, 9.5 metres (31 feet) wide and 8–9 metre (26–29½ feet) high, and these were positioned every 5.3 metres (17½ feet) along the wall. Drains set into the base of the wall allowed rainwater running off the plateau to escape.

The new town was also organized into slightly off-square blocks, but these were more than twice as large as those in the old town. Most of the streets were wider and the houses were larger, with between one and five rooms. There is evidence that more activities were going on in the domestic spaces, as more commodities were available to the inhabitants. In particular, many counterweights for presses have been found. Chemical analysis of residues from jars and the floors of houses indicate that these presses were for producing olive oil, so it looks as though the people of Entremont had developed a significant cottage industry.

The biggest building of the new town backed onto the line of the old town wall, which had been destroyed and recycled. It was a monumental hypostyle hall, 20 metres (65½ feet) long and 5 metres (16½ feet) wide, with a series of wooden pillars supporting a second storey. The walls were made of stone in the lower courses and packed clay in the upper, with a timber-framed façade. The pillars of the façade rested upon a long stone bar, or *stylobate*, which included stones previously used in the primitive sanctuary that predated the settlement. Twenty skulls pierced with holes have been found scattered around the *stylobate*, suggesting that the façade was decorated with heads nailed to the timbers. The floor of the building was fine-packed clay, while the internal walls were coated with white lime. The street in front of the hall was enlarged and the effect was to create an impressive public building set apart from the rest of the town. Although admittedly probably based on Greek models, which the Salyens would have seen in Massalia or other colonies, this building is a remarkable symbol of Gallic sophistication and ability.

The Cult of the Heroes

Arguably the most important parts of the settlement were the four religious sanctuaries. These are marked by carved *stelae* and lintels, sculptures, statues and skulls. Some of the lintels have recesses for heads or skulls, alongside reliefs of heads. The sculptures show heroic figures, seated in Buddha-like poses, with weapons and trophies, including skulls. The heads and skulls might represent either trophies of the dead or relics of revered ancestors.

Such idols and votive figures have a long history going back to the beginnings of Gallic culture, but at Entremont the context in which they are displayed speaks of changing social structures. Although Celtic society is traditionally renowned as an egalitarian one, the evidence of this and other sites is that it was becoming much more stratified, with aristocratic lineages asserting their superiority and dominant status. In the Entremont sanctuaries the heroes are displayed in close association with representations of these aristocratic lineages, suggesting that the ruling classes were trying to appropriate the pre-existing cult of the hero to bolster their own prestige and status. Historians believe that the influence of the Greco-Roman trade via Massalia, which brought wealth and luxury goods, may have helped to drive this social shift.

The End of Entremont

During the Punic Wars between Carthage and Rome, Massalia supported Rome, and later, when their colonies were threatened by the Salyens and others, the colonists appealed to Rome, the rising power in the western Mediterranean, for help. The price of this assistance was acceptance of Roman hegemony. Italian merchants took over trade through Massalia, which increasingly dealt with imports from Italy.

In 125 BCE Roman forces moved against the troublesome Salyens, but Entremont, probably the Salyen capital, resisted the legions. In 123 BCE, under the Roman

consul C. Sextius Calvinus, another force besieged the city, which is littered with evidence of the savage onslaught, including stone balls hurled by catapults, iron bolts fired by giant *ballistae* (crossbows) and the heads of many Roman *pilae* (javelins). The defenders left their own traces – clay slingshot balls, iron daggers, arrows and spears. But Roman military might was too much and the city was taken and sacked, as the remains of broken amphorae attest. In a few of the houses, small caches of coins, jewellery and other valuables buried in the mud floors eluded discovery by the rapacious legionnaires.

According to ancient sources the Saluvian king and his nobles fled to the north and took refuge with a tribe called the Allobriges, while the surviving inhabitants of

A close-up of a furnace for metal production, one of the more sophisticated activities carried out in the Old Town, which was a much more primitive settlement than its replacement displaying little more than subsistence activity.

Entremont were deported (possibly into slavery), with the exception of a nobleman called Craton, a Roman collaborator. Along with 900 of his people he was allowed to remain at Entremont, where they apparently lived until c 90 BCE, when a second military destruction suggests that Craton's descendants did not maintain their cordial relations with the Romans. After this the site was abandoned, while a new Roman town founded nearby (now Aix-en-Provence) flourished.

AFRICA

The five cities in this chapter span a vast gulf of history, from the 11th century BCE to the 15th century CE. But they also span a cultural gulf, between the super-Saharan world of the famous civilizations of antiquity and the sub-Saharan world that remains little known and poorly understood. The former is the familiar world of the ancient Egyptians, Greeks and Romans, in which the extraordinarily long narrative of Egyptian history, represented here through the tale of the lost city of Tanis, gives way to the Classical world, and the famous names of Alexandria, a Greek city with an Egyptian flavour, and Leptis Magna, one of the best preserved of all Roman cities.

The sub-Saharan world has its own rich history, with its own narrative of the rise and fall of empires, but the lack of written sources, combined with the relative paucity of archaeological research, means that this narrative is largely unknown. The haunting site of Great Zimbabwe offers a rare window on this untold history, although it took the efforts of unbiased and professional archaeologists to start to unravel its mystery, for, like several sites covered in this book (see, for instance, Cahokia on page 148 and Tiwanaku on page 174), it has been subject to interpretation (or misinterpretation) through ideologically rather than scientifically motivated research.

The two worlds are bridged by the ancient city of Meroe and the venerable Kushite civilization of which it was capital. The Kushites are rarely seen as much more than adjuncts to their more famous neighbour to the north, Egypt, but in practice they represent a coming together of the super- and sub-Saharan worlds. Initially they developed in imitation of the Egyptians, but the establishment of Meroe signalled a geopolitical shift towards the sub-Saharan world and the development of a new, uniquely sub-Saharan culture.

Corinthian columns at Leptis Magna, in Libya, one of the best preserved Roman cities.

GREAT ZIMBABWE

LOCATION: ZIMBABWE

DATE OF CONSTRUCTION: *c* 13TH CENTURY CE

ABANDONED: LATE 15TH CENTURY CE

BUILT BY: MWENE MUTAPA EMPIRE

KEY FEATURES: GREAT ENCLOSURE; SOPHISTICATED
DRY-STONE MASONRY; CONICAL TOWER; HILLTOP
COMPLEX; STONE BIRDS

The greatest archaeological site in sub-Saharan Africa and perhaps the only one to lend its name to a modern-day state, Great Zimbabwe was once the centre of a mighty trading empire. Its ruins have inspired exotic speculations and been at the centre of political storms.

Great Zimbabwe is the collective name given to a group of ruins spread across a valley and adjoining hills on the Zimbabwe Plateau – a region of high ground between the Zambezi and Limpopo rivers in southern Africa. It was designated a UNESCO World Heritage Site in 1986. Its most prominent and best-known feature is a circular wall known as the Great Enclosure, a feat of sophisticated monumental masonry that continues to awe and inspire today as it must have when it was first constructed, probably during the 13th–15th centuries CE.

This was the height of the Mwene Mutapa Empire (known by Europeans as Monomotapa), a kingdom of the Shona (the peoples who still live in the area) that developed from about 900 CE. At first the empire was based on cattle herding, but from around 1100 Mwene Mutapa took over control of the lucrative trading networks that linked ivory, iron and gold production centres inland with the merchants on the coast, who brought in return luxury goods from the Middle and Far East. Goods found at the site include silk, cotton, Chinese porcelain, Persian faience, glass from Syria and beads from India. In particular, rich gold fields were opened up to the west of Great Zimbabwe and considerable wealth flowed through the hands of the king, or *mambo*. It was this wealth that funded construction of Great Zimbabwe's monumental masonry and attracted a growing population.

The Hill Complex

The whole complex covers about 728 hectares (1,800 acres), but the ruins are concentrated at three main sites. Atop a rocky hill sits the group known as the Hill Complex, which includes an oval stone enclosure about 100 metres (330 feet) across at its widest point and up to 11 metres (36 feet) high, within which sit a number of huts and small buildings made of *daga* – mud, gravel and earth from termite mounds, mixed to give a sort of concrete, which forms the most common building material in Africa. The hill was probably the part of the site that was occupied earliest. Remains indicate that it was first settled by Iron Age herders and farmers as early as the 5th century CE, probably attracted by the area's rich grazing, fertile soil and, thanks to its altitude, relative lack of tsetse-fly spreading sleeping sickness. When Great Zimbabwe became rich and powerful, the Hill Complex was developed into the enclave of the *mambo* and possibly other figures of power, such as priests. A number of stone birds perched on top of stone pillars were found inside the complex, one of which has since become the national emblem of Zimbabwe.

The Great Enclosure

Below the Hill Complex is the most iconic and impressive of Great Zimbabwe's wonders – the Great Enclosure, known by the 19th-century residents of the area as the *Imbahuru*, which means either 'great house' or 'house of the great woman' in the local Karanga dialect of Shona. This latter translation would prove to have significant resonance for early European interpretations of the site. The Great Enclosure is an elliptical space enclosed by a giant wall with a circumference of 244 metres (735 feet), which is up to 11 metres (33 feet) high in places. It is constructed of two layers of rectangular granite blocks, laid together with such precision that no mortar was required, filled with earth and stones. The wall is about half as thick at the base as it is high and tapers in towards the top. Almost one million blocks were used in its construction. The blocks come from the surrounding hills, where granite domes erode through a process known as exfoliation, whereby thin sheets of rock peel off and natural heating and cooling cause these to crack along existing fault lines to give handy brick-shaped blocks. The medieval Shona people would accelerate the process by artificially heating and cooling the granite and by driving wooden wedges into cracks.

Notable features of the Great Enclosure include an inner wall that runs around part of the main wall to create a 55-metre (180-foot) long alley, openings and doorways, smoothly rounded walls and rounded steps crafted with great skill. Inside the enclosure is a solid conical tower 9 metres (30 feet) high, a number of standing stones and traces of many *daga* huts.

The Valley Ruins

Scattered through the valley that surrounds the Great Enclosure are the ruins of many smaller stone enclosures and traces of more *daga* huts. These structures are the youngest and archaeologists speculate that they were built to accommodate the swelling population of Great Zimbabwe as its power and wealth drew in greater and greater numbers. At its height the population may have reached 17–19,000, equivalent to that of medieval London. One of the enclosures is thought to have been where the wives of the *mambo* lived – there may have been up to 1,000 of them.

The layout of the site had socio-political aspects. The physical separation and elevation of the Hill Complex mirrored and demonstrated the status of the king, while lesser chiefs of the kingdom maintained smaller enclosures of their own on less elevated points and the common people spread around the valley. When the population was at its height, Great Zimbabwe would have been a busy metropolis, with traders bringing in raw materials for craftsmen to process and farmers and herders keeping them supplied with food. The function of the Great Enclosure itself, however, remains something of a mystery. It is thought that it may have been a royal palace or played a role in initiation rites and/or religious ceremonies. Part of the wall is decorated with a frieze of chevrons, thought to have sexual symbolism, while the conical tower is an obvious phallic symbol that may have been a symbolic replica of Shona grain storage structures.

Overleaf: The conical tower in the Great Enclosure, possibly a giant phallic symbol, but also thought to be a symbolic replica of a grain store. No mortar is used to hold together the stone blocks.

View of part of the 55-metre (180-foot) long alley that runs between the inner and outer walls of the Grand Enclosure. Note the skill and precision of the dry stone masonry. The function of the alley is unclear – perhaps it was defensive, or perhaps it had some ritual function linked to the greater religious symbolism of the whole site.

King Solomon's Mines

The city began to diminish from the mid–late 15th century, probably because the gold fields that underpinned its wealth began to run dry, but possibly also because the area could not support the environmental demands – particularly firewood and grazing – of the population. It was almost entirely deserted by the time that European explorers began to penetrate the interior of the continent, although subsequently there may have been low-level reoccupation of parts of the site and the Great Enclosure was still used for religious ceremonies. This meant the largely empty city was available as a template for the assumptions and preoccupations of European explorers and treasure-hunters.

The first Europeans to report the existence of the site were the Portuguese, who had set up trading forts on the East African coast to access gold, ivory and the other riches of the continent, but who did not penetrate inland. Native informants told them of the rich gold mines of the empire of Monomotapa and of its great fortresses called Symbaoe (possibly a misinterpretation of 'Zimbabwe'), built of stones joined without mortar. The Portuguese and subsequent Europeans connected Monomotapa with the legendary Ophir, said in the Bible to be the home of the Queen of Sheba and the location of the gold mines that were the source of King Solomon's fabulous wealth.

By the mid-19th century, European explorers and missionaries finally penetrated the interior. In 1870 eccentric German explorer Karl Mauch (who typically eschewed the use of porters or bearers and carried all his gear himself, while dressed in a suit of antelope hide leather and sporting a large umbrella as a sunshade) heard tales of Monomotapa from a missionary and determined to win glory – and possibly riches – as the discoverer of Ophir. After various tribulations he reached the site and found the evidence he sought. Chipping a piece of wood from the lintel of a doorway he decided that it resembled his pencil, made from cedar, and must therefore have come from Lebanon. To his mind this confirmed the obvious: such marvellous structures could not have been built by Africans, but must have been constructed by Phoenicians, ancient inhabitants of Lebanon. He went further, speculating that the Hilltop Complex was the Queen of Sheba's attempt to replicate Solomon's Temple.

Alas for Mauch, a search of the site revealed neither gold nor gemstones, while his discoveries were greeted with relative indifference back in Europe. He died in relative obscurity five years later, after falling from a window back in his native land.

Whitewash

This extraordinary and completely unfounded interpretation of the site was to dominate subsequent European conceptions. At the end of the 19th century the land around Zimbabwe fell into the hands of Cecil Rhodes, whose project for a British-dominated Africa required certain basic ideological and anthropological assumptions, namely that Africans were barbarous savages incapable of civilization and that it was the 'white man's burden' to lift them out of their benighted state.

The British archaeologists dispatched to survey Great Zimbabwe confirmed Mauch's earlier theory. The city had clearly been built by Phoenicians or other Mediterranean visitors, concluded James Bent in his 1892 book *The Ruined Cities of Mashonaland*, which inspired H. Rider Haggard's adventure novel *King Solomon's Mines*. Bent's successor, Richard N. Hall, was incompetent and destructive, clearing 3.5 metres (12 feet) of soil and rubble from the ruins in an attempt to 'restore' them and thus irreparably damaging the archaeological record.

In subsequent decades the area became the country of Rhodesia and Great Zimbabwe became an ideological battleground. For the white elite governing Rhodesia it was important that the ruins should have a non-African background, but as early as 1905 the archaeologist David Randall-MacIver compared finds at the site with the prevalent use of identical artefacts and technology by the Shona peoples still living in the area. He drew the obvious conclusion: Great Zimbabwe had been built by Africans, probably by essentially the same people that still lived there. Archaeologist Gertrude Caton-Thompson, sent to disprove his findings, instead proved them accurate.

The Rhodesian authorities would not accept this line. A cavalcade of eccentric theories was advanced, linking the ruins with everyone from the pharaohs and the Lost Tribes of Israel to the Vikings. Access to the site for Africans was restricted and government archaeologists were fired for straying from the party line. Meanwhile the ruins became a key symbol for the African independence movement and when the country finally broke free of its apartheid system the nation's name was changed to reflect this (although there is disagreement over which dialect of Shona 'Zimbabwe' actually derives from and thus whether it means 'houses of stone' or 'venerated houses'). Today Great Zimbabwe remains a politically charged place; a national monument that helps to define Zimbabwe's cultural identity, but also a focus of grievances over the nation's troubled colonial history.

TANIS

LOCATION: NILE DELTA, EGYPT

DATE OF CONSTRUCTION: *c* 1070 BCE

ABANDONED: PRE-7TH CENTURY CE

BUILT BY: PHARAOH SMENDES AND THE TWENTY-FIRST AND TWENTY-SECOND DYNASTIES

KEY FEATURES: RE-USE OF BLOCKS AND STATUARY FROM OLDER SITES; TEMPLE COMPOUND WITH WALL; TEMPLE OF AMUN; ROYAL TOMBS AND TREASURES

Scattered blocks and the stumps of obelisks litter the top of a huge sand mound, marooned along the former course of a long-since silted-up branch of the Nile Delta. Here was the site of Tanis, one-time capital of ancient Egypt and the site of the only authentically undisturbed royal tombs, the extraordinary though unheralded contents of which rival the glories of Tutankhamun.

Tanis is the Greek name for the ancient Egyptian city of Djanet, a site known today as San el-Hagar – 'the place of stones'. Technically speaking, San el-Hagar actually refers to the northernmost and larger of two huge sand mounds or *gezira*: it rises over 30 metres (98½ feet) above the surrounding flood plain and has an area of 177 hectares (437 acres). From around the 11th century BCE until the late 8th century BCE it was capital of Egypt (albeit one of several at some points). Before and after this it was an important regional capital and as well as its administrative role it was a major religious and trading centre, funnelling trans-Mediterranean trade into and out of Egypt, until its branch of the Nile silted up and it was left high and dry. Despite this prominence, the circumstances of its construction made Tanis extremely difficult for latter-day archaeologists to identify, for the site is a kind of structural palimpsest, composed of the building blocks of other cities and other times.

Delta Pharaohs and Southern High Priests

Tanis was the product of a confused and divisive period of ancient Egyptian politics. The Twentieth Dynasty was weak and failing and in Upper Egypt (the southern part of the country) the pharaoh had lost most real power to the high priests of Amun in the city of Thebes. By the end of the reign of Ramesses XI, last pharaoh of the Twentieth Dynasty, the High Priest Herihor was openly sharing power as co-ruler. The rise of the high priests saw the pharaonic power base shift to the north of Egypt in the Nile Delta region, where the city of Pi-Ramesses had been made capital. At the death of Ramesses XI, the throne passed to the govenor of Tanis, one Smendes, who may have been Ramesses' son-in-law. As his residence he took Tanis, superseding Pi-Ramesses, whose own branch of the Nile was now drying up.

Smendes' Twenty-First Dynasty had Libyan connections, which became more marked with the transition to the Twenty-Second Dynasty under Shoshenq I, which retained Tanis as its seat. However, in the mid-9th century BCE the south of Egypt broke away to become a separate kingdom, and by the 8th century BCE several rival dynasties were established, running concurrently and each ruling a portion of Egypt; Tanis was now only the capital of a small local kingdom.

Egypt was reunited by a Nubian dynasty around 720 BCE (see Meroe page 106), and Tanis henceforth reverted to the role of a provinical capital.

With only intermittent control of the country and much civil strife, the view of the dynasties of the Third Intermediate Period has traditionally been that they were poor shadows of former glories, scraping by in pale imitation of the wealth and opulent splendour of the preceding New Kingdom. Discoveries made at Tanis were to both reinforce and undermine this accepted view.

Below: Part of a stele from the temple compound (also known as the Sanctuary) at Tanis. It shows the pharaoh Ramesses II making an offering to a god. This stele was recycled by the constructors of Tanis from the ruins of the nearby city of Pi-Ramesses, founded by Ramesses II. Such recycling initially caused Egyptologists to misidentify Tanis as Pi-Ramesses.

Overleaf: Remounted blocks and statues at Tanis, demonstrating why the mound containing the remnants of the city came to be called San el-Hagar, the Place of Stones.

Decoding Tanis

The first archaeology at Tanis was little more than looting, with quantities of statuary carted off to European capitals. But Egyptologists such as Auguste Mariette and Flinders Petrie also uncovered inscriptions, statues and names dating back to the Middle Kingdom and the Twelfth Dynasty (c 1900 BCE), as well as ones that seemed to identify the site as the lost city of Avaris, which was later re-named Pi-Ramesses.

When French Egyptologist Pierre Montet began what was to be the most significant exploration of the site in 1929, he also found similar evidence. But later Egyptologists have realized that Montet and his predecessors were wrong and that the inscriptions were misleading: the blocks and statuary were recycled – moved from elsewhere and pressed into service. It is now clear that the nearby, but probably largely abandoned, city of Pi-Ramesses had served as a sort of quarry for the builders of Tanis. Other blocks, obelisks and statues came from other locations. Some dated back as far as the Old Kingdom. This evidence of a capital cobbled together from the recycled detritus of older cities would appear to tie in with the traditional view of the impoverished Intermediate dynasties. However, it may have been that the northern delta kings did not have access to the quarries of Upper Egypt when they built their new capital and were simply being practical.

Excavations have revealed that the primary feature of the city was a massive wall of mud brick, which enclosed a sandy bowl between four raised areas on the San el-Hagar mound, creating a huge temple compound. The wall was 10 metres (33 feet) high and 15 metres (49 feet) thick. It was built by Psusennes I, third pharaoh of the Twenty-First Dynasty (reign 1039–991 BCE), in an apparent effort to create a northern Thebes. Thebes was the religious capital of Egypt, with a complex of temples to the 'divine family' – Amun, Mut and Khonsu. Its importance as the focus of Egyptian religious and cultural life

brought power and prestige. Psusennes created his own temple complex with shrines to the divine family and then went further and created a northern analogue of Thebes's Valley of the Kings – the sacred valley where the great pharaohs of ages past had been interred (see Tombs to Rival Tutankhamun below).

Other structures that have been identified include smaller temples (chapels) built by later pharaohs. After the Persian occupation of Egypt (525–405 BCE), Nectanebo I of the Thirtieth Dynasty (reign 380–362 BCE) initiated a new programme of building at Tanis. He built a new, enormous mud-brick enclosure and started new temples, as well as constructing a sacred lake in the northern corner of the city. Egypt soon fell again to the Persians and then to Alexander the Great and afterwards was ruled by the Greco-Egyptian Ptolemies. They completed some of these unfinished temples, but by now the original great temple to Amun was gone, its site built over with houses.

The Ptolemies gave way to the Romans, but by the end of the Roman Era the branch of the Nile that gave Tanis its raison d'être had silted up and it was – like Pi-Ramesses before it – defunct and largely abandoned by the time of the Islamic conquest. Lime burners destroyed much of the fabric of the city, leaving little but the granite blocks and obelisks that litter the site today.

Tombs to Rival Tutankhamun

The unprepossessing detritus of ancient Tanis on the surface concealed something spectacular beneath. Howard Carter's discovery of the tomb of Tutankhamun in the Valley of the Kings had electrified the world of archaeology with its astonishing collection of grave goods, but even King Tutankhamun's tomb had not escaped the attentions of ancient tomb raiders. Reapplied seals on the doors, chests with contents that did not match the inventories listed on their exteriors and the general disarray of parts of the tomb all indicated that it had been broken into and robbed in antiquity, before being resealed and later lost to the world. Tanis, however, hosted a mini-Valley of the Kings and included a royal tomb that had never been disturbed, complete with all its grave goods – treasures to rival those of Tutankhamun.

In 1939, in his eleventh season of excavation at Tanis, and with the gathering clouds of war in faraway Europe casting a long shadow over his endeavours, Montet unearthed a tomb within the temple precinct. Inscriptions identified it as that of Osorkon II (ruler during the Twenty-Second Dynasty 872–837 BCE) and although it had been long plundered, the thieves had left behind heavy objects such as a stunning quartzite sarcophagus, *shabtis* (tomb statues supposed to come to life in the afterlife as servants for the dead pharaoh) and alabaster jars for his internal organs.

Far more impressive was the adjoining tomb, which proved to be undisturbed. Nested within a granite sarcophagus and a granite coffin was a coffin of solid silver; within lay incredible jewellery and a glorious face-mask of solid gold (the mummy itself had largely decomposed). Although the inscriptions on the wall attributed the tomb to Psusennes I, who had originally built it for himself and his queen Mutnodjmet, there were numerous other burials in the five-chambered tomb, including three more Twenty-First Dynasty pharoahs, General Wendebauenjed (an important military man), and the previously unknown pharaoh Shoshenq II (ruler during Twenty-Second Dynasty), who occupied an unusual silver coffin with a head shaped like a falcon.

In all Montet discovered six tombs, which hosted the burials of at least 14 royals and nobles. The exquisite treasures, including face-masks of workmanship at least as fine as that of Tutankhamun, and fabulous jewellery of gold and lapis lazuli (not to mention sets of golden sandals to protect the feet of kings on the road to the afterlife), show that the kings of the Intermediate Period were far from impoverished. Yet

the tombs also show the continuing practice of reusing materials. Sarcophagus lids were carved from statues, while a huge granite block used to plug the entrance to one of the tombs had originally been part of an obelisk in praise of Ramesses II. The use of a sarcophagus from Thebes reminds us that Psusennes' brother was High Priest at Thebes and was apparently responsible for state-sanctioned looting of the Valley of the Kings.

Montet's discoveries, which included no less than five intact and undisturbed royal mummies, made in 1939 and 1940, were overshadowed by the war in Europe and never got the publicity that attended Carter's success. Today the wonders of Tanis sit in Cairo Museum, often overlooked by tourists eager to see the more celebrated treasures of Tutankhamun.

TANIS AND THE LOST ARK

The name of Tanis is probably best known today as the hiding place of the Ark of the Covenant in the blockbuster movie *Raiders of the Lost Ark*, which presents an entirely fanciful and inaccurate picture of the city. Most scholars dismiss this link as a convenient fiction, invented by the moviemakers to justify an exotic Egyptian location. There is, however, a genuine if tenuous link between Tanis and the Ark, for the Bible speaks of an Egyptian king called Shishak who invaded Israel and took Jerusalem. One theory about the missing Ark is that it was looted from the Temple of Solomon by Shishak. Could Shishak have been Shoshenq of Tanis? This was thought to be the case for many years (although more recently the link has been disputed), in which case perhaps the Ark was stolen away to Tanis, just as Indiana Jones discovered.

MEROE

LOCATION: SUDAN
DATE OF CONSTRUCTION: *c* 750 BCE
ABANDONED: *c* 350 CE
BUILT BY: KUSHITES
KEY FEATURES: PYRAMIDS; TEMPLES OF AMUN AND
APEDEMAK; ROYAL BATHS; BRONZE HEAD OF AUGUSTUS

Beyond the borders of ancient Egypt another civilization rose and fell and rose again, lasting almost half as long as that of the Egyptian pharoahs and producing fabulous arts and crafts and distinctive architecture of its own, yet it has kept very much below the popular historical radar. The Kingdom of Kush had, for much of its history, its capital at ancient Meroe, a city fabled by ancient authors and marked by its distinctive pyramids and exotic tomb treasures, but which met its end in an industrial-ecological crisis that offers a stark warning to our modern world.

The Land of Kush

The kingdom to the south of ancient Egypt has gone by many different names, but is best known as Kush (sometimes Cush), in the land of the Nubians. Here along the upper reaches of the Nile, from the First Cataract down to the far south, in what is now Sudan, Africans built a long-lasting civilization that both drew inspiration from and contended with the mighty Egypt in a relationship characterized by constant struggle and occasional fruitfulness.

The first Kushite kingdom from around 2400 BCE centred on Kerma, relatively far down the Nile (i.e. to the north, nearer ancient Egypt). It was able to flourish during a period of relative instability and weakness in its powerful neighbour, but when new dynasties re-established control over Egypt they also regained their dominance over the lands to the south. Kush was a valuable source of agricultural products and, crucially, gold. New Kingdom (1539–1075 BCE) pharaohs took hundreds of kilograms of gold in tribute from Kush each year. Later phases of Kushite development saw its centre shift further away from Egypt and towards sub-Saharan Africa, initially geographically when the Egyptians reasserted control and moved the capital south to Napata, and later culturally as well, when the capital eventually moved to Meroe.

The collapse of the New Kingdom and the disarray of Egypt's Third Intermediate Period (see Tanis page 100), once again allowed Kush to develop as an independent kingdom, with its capital at Napata and a dynastic cemetery established at the nearby site of El-Kurru. The power of this Napatan kingdom grew until Nubian kings were dictating terms to the Egyptians, culminating in Kushites taking complete control of Egypt and establishing the Twenty-Fifth Dynasty, which ruled, at first in tandem with northern dynasties and later in sole power, from 747–656 BCE.

Meroe's distinctive pyramids. In their very steep angle they were inspired by Egyptian private tombs of the New Kingdom (1550–1070 BCE), rather than by the classic royal pyramids of Egypt's Old and Middle Kingdoms (27th to 17th centuries BCE)

The Rise of Meroe

Invasion by the Assyrians and later, re-establishment of native Egyptian dynasty, forced the Kushites back into their own lands and attempts by Kushite kings to reconquer territory to the north were repulsed. From around 750 BCE the city of Meroe (on the east bank of the Nile, about 200 kilometres (124 miles) northeast of modern-day Khartoum) had become an important administrative centre for the south of Kush and when the Egyptian pharaoh Psametik II raided far into Kushite territory in 591 BCE, sacking Napata, its strategic benefits became more obvious. The Kushite king Aspelta relocated the royal court to Meroe, although the royal burial ground remained at Nuri, close to Napata, where it had been established around 690 BCE. Eventually, around 270 BCE, the royal burial grounds were also relocated to Meroe, and it remained the capital of Kush until around 350 CE.

A rich and powerful city far to the south of territory familiar to the Egyptians and the successive masters of Egypt – the Persians, the Greeks and eventually the Romans – Meroe became a fabled land. The Persian emperor Cambyses sent a huge expeditionary force up the Nile, lured by the promise of great booty, but it turned back, defeated by the harsh terrain. Classical writers such as Herodotus and Diodorus Siculus spoke of Meroe in terms of wonder. It was said to sit on a great island in the Nile, possibly reflecting the fact that in reality it was surrounded on three sides by water.

The Ptolemies managed to maintain the integrity of Egypt's borders and keep Kush at bay. They were succeeded by the Romans, with whom the Kushites enjoyed a relationship rivalled only by the Parthians for longevity. The two empires got off to a bad start in 23 BCE, when the brutal suppression by Rome of a rebellion of mainly Nubian subjects triggered a Kushite raid in which a

Bas reliefs at the Meroe pyramids, showing a procession of figures personifying the produce of the royal estates.

statue of Augustus was torn down, its bronze head removed and buried beneath the entrance to a temple in Meroe, so that everyone crossing the threshold would symbolically trample upon it. The head was recovered in 1912 by British archaeologists excavating Meroe and now sits in the British Museum in London, testament to Kushite ability to match Rome in force of arms. To avenge this insult a force under the prefect Gaius Petronius penetrated deep into Kush, sacking Napata and taking thousands of slaves, but Kushite resistance eventually forced the Romans to retreat behind their borders and they never threatened Meroe again.

City of Industry

The pre-eminence of Meroe was largely economic. One of the economic foundations of Kush was its iron industry. It was rich in ore and manufactured iron for export as well as domestic use. For instance, iron tools helped increase agricultural productivity, allowing Kush to develop a mixed farming economy that made full use of the tropical wet season, as well as providing weapons to its formidable armed forces. Meroe was the centre of iron smelting, supplied with water from the Nile and, crucially, a rich source of wood for charcoal production in the form of dense acacia groves. It has been described as the 'Birmingham of ancient Africa', attested to by ancient slag heaps, such as the one on which Meroe's Lion Temple sits.

Trade in iron but also gold, domestic products such as cotton textiles, and commodities from far-flung parts of Africa was another source of wealth. In the early days of Kush, trade depended on passage up the Nile to the Mediterranean and thence to the rich markets of the ancient world, but as its centre shifted south, so new trade routes independent of Egypt opened up. The north-south trade route was superseded by an east-west axis. The growth of trade routes along the Red Sea, mediated by Greek and Nabatean merchants (see Petra

page 34), cut out the need to travel via the Nile, while the increasing use of camels from the 2nd century BCE opened caravan routes extending across the whole of sub-Saharan Africa. Meroe became part of a lucrative trade network stretching from West Africa to India and China.

Pools and Pyramids

Meroe may have been home to up to 25,000 people. Excavations have revealed the remains of a quay by the river, several palaces and a number of temples, including both Egyptian ones (the biggest temple was to the chief Egyptian god Amun) and indigenous ones, such as the lion-headed Apedemak. One notable find – a brick-lined pool 7 metres (23 feet) square and 3 metres (10 feet) deep with lion-headed spouts around the sides – was labelled the Royal Baths by the colonial era archaeologists, and although aspects of Meroitic Kushite culture were influenced by the Hellenistic powers to the north, this description may reflect typical colonial chauvinistic attitudes i.e. the assumption that an African culture must have borrowed or copied European models. It is now thought that the 'baths' may actually have been a water shrine of some sort or even a swimming pool.

The primary cultural and religious influence on Kush was undoubtedly Egyptian. The most notable expression of this influence was in the adoption of pyramids for the royal tombs, although the very steep angle of Kushite pyramids was inspired by Egyptian private tombs of the New Kingdom (1550–1070 BCE), rather than by the classic royal pyramids of Egypt's Old and Middle Kingdoms (27th to 17th centuries BCE).

When the tombs were excavated in the 19th and early 20th centuries, no mummies were found (they may not have survived or the Kushites may not have practiced mummification), but rich troves of grave goods were uncovered. Most spectacular of all were the finds of the treasure hunter Giuseppe Ferlini in 1834, who destroyed many pyramids in his hunt for loot, but successfully uncovered the tomb treasures of Queen Amanishakheto, including much exquisitely crafted jewellery.

After the capital moved to Meroe, Kushite culture became increasingly African and the tomb treasures of Meroe help to illustrate this cultural evolution. According to Dr Salah el-Din Muhammed Ahmed, director of fieldwork at the National Museum in Khartoum, 'From the graves and from the images painted on tombs we can see that people looked much more African than Mediterranean. The jewellery is really of an African nature – like anklets, bracelets, ear studs and earrings – and you can still find the style of the jewellery used by the Meroites on tribes of the savannah belt south of Khartoum.'

The Line of Queens

One of the most intriguing features of ancient Meroitic Kush was the importance of its queens, known via the Greeks as *kandakes*, which in turn was mistaken as the personal name 'Candace' by some ancient writers. The *kandake* shared power with a *qore*, or king, but he was often a purely ceremonial figure, while his consort was commander-in-chief, prime minister and chief priestess. She might even lead the armies of Kush into battle. One famous legend tells of how Alexander the Great led his armies to the walls of Meroe but halted and turned back when confronted by Queen Candace and her legions. Probably the most famous *kandake* was Amanirenas, who ruled from *c* 40–*c* 10 BCE and led numerous campaigns against the Romans, eventually forcing them to limit their ambitions for conquest and guaranteeing Kushite independence for another three centuries.

The End of Meroe

Exactly what happened to Meroe is unclear. Traditionally it was thought that the rising power of the kingdom of Aksum (also Axum) in Ethiopia led to the decline of Kush and that Meroe fell to the invading Akumsite king Ezana *c* 350 CE. A *stele* erected at Meroe

AMANIRENAS

The Kushite *kandake* Amanirenas was a formidable queen and a courageous general. When the Romans imposed their control on the stretch of the Nile between Egypt and Kush, Amanirenas and her son led an army north to capture the territory, enslave the populace and carry off the statue of Augustus. In defending Kush against Gaius Petronius's punitive expedition she lost an eye, but succeeded in halting the Roman advance. Eventually the Romans were forced to sue for peace, the emperor Augustus himself meeting with her representatives. According to legend, they presented him with a bundle of arrows and the message, 'The *kandake* sends you these arrows. If you want peace they are a token of her friendship and warmth. If you want war, you are going to need them.'

bears testament to his triumph. But it is now generally believed that Meroe was already largely abandoned by this time and that by then the region was mainly inhabited by the pastoral Noba tribe. So what had happened to the glories of Meroe and its thriving population?

The rise of Aksum may well have contributed to the decline of Meroe, by cutting its access to the lucrative trade routes of the Red Sea, but historians now suspect that Meroe's iron industry was the true culprit. Extensive deforestation to produce the charcoal needed to fire the furnaces may have led to ecological collapse. Top soil eroded, rainfall declined and the region became arid and unproductive. In combination with the failure of the trade routes and pressure from the Noba, this was too much for Meroitic Kush and it collapsed. Ancient Meroe stands as one of the world's first examples of a civilization destroyed by untrammelled industrial development.

ALEXANDRIA

LOCATION: NILE DELTA, EGYPT

DATE OF CONSTRUCTION: 331 BCE

ABANDONED: NOT ABANDONED

BUILT BY: ALEXANDER THE GREAT; PTOLEMAIC PHARAOHS

KEY FEATURES: LIGHTHOUSE OF PHAROS; MUSEUM AND ROYAL LIBRARY; SERAPEUM; SOMA (TOMB OF ALEXANDER AND THE PTOLEMIES); CATACOMBS OF KOM EL SHOQAFA

Known as the Pearl of the Mediterranean, Alexandria was one of the greatest and most remarkable cities in the world for a thousand years. It was a place of contradictions – a city of great learning and fundamentalist bigotry; cosmopolitan in the extreme and intolerant in the extreme; the greatest Greek city in history, but Egyptian; home to a multitude of great buildings – including hundreds of palaces and temples and several Wonders of the World, including the Lighthouse, the Great Library, Alexander's Tomb and the Catacombs of Kom el Shoqafa, yet apparently barren of physical heritage; a huge, sprawling present-day metropolis, but a lost city in the truest sense.

City on the Edge

On Egypt's Mediterranean coast, on a strip of land between Lake Mareotis and the sea, lies Egypt's second city and its largest port, Alexandria. The modern city bears few traces of the ancient metropolis that in its heyday was one of the largest cities in the world and arguably the greatest. It was founded by and named for Alexander the Great. Having conquered Egypt and desirous of consolidating his power and reinforcing maritime and trade links between the Nile Valley and Greece and Asia, he chose one of the few suitable harbour sites on the Mediterranean coast, renowned

enough for its natural advantages to be mentioned by Homer in the *Odyssey*. Book Four records that, 'Therein is a harbour with good anchorage, whence men launch the shapely ships into the sea...' The island of Pharos just offshore shielded the coast, while it was far enough away from the mouths of the Nile to be free of silt.

A small Egyptian town called Rhakotis occupied part of the site, but in around 331 BCE Alexander marked out the basic layout of a new city – according to legend using grain when other materials were not available, such was his eagerness to get the project started – and employed the architect Dinocrates to elaborate. The city was laid out in classical Greek style, with orthogonal streets (running at right angles to give a grid pattern) oriented to the shoreline and based around two main axes: the east-west Canopus Street, running from the Moon Gate in the east to the Sun Gate in the west and the north-south Soma Street, running from Lake Mareotis to the shore, at a point where a causeway called the Heptastadion was built to link Pharos to the mainland and create a harbour on each side.

Alexander did not stay to see his city built, setting off for fresh adventures and conquests and dying in Babylon in 323 BCE. Africa and the prize kingdom of Egypt were ultimately seized by his general, Ptolemy, thus founding the Ptolemaic Dynasty that was to shape Alexandria. In the power struggle that followed the great king's death his corpse was a potent counter/bargaining chip and Ptolemy hijacked the lavish funeral cortège on its way back to Macedon, bringing Alexander's body to Egypt where it was initially interred at Memphis. According to legend Ptolemy was also motivated by an oracle that the land where Alexander was buried would become the richest kingdom in the world.

Later Alexander's body was brought to Alexandria and placed in a tomb at the intersection of the two main streets, a location known as the Soma or Sema (meaning 'the body' in ancient Greek). It became one of the great tourist attractions of the ancient world, drawing famous visitors such as Julius Caesar, Augustus (who allegedly broke the preserved corpse's nose when he leant over it) and a succession of other Roman emperors. The location of the tomb remains a great unsolved mystery, although modern legend has it that it might be located beneath the Nebi Daniel Mosque; however, there is absolutely no real evidence for this idea.

As the capital of the Hellenistic rulers of Egypt, Alexandria had a unique character from the start. It was Greek in design and many other aspects, with a mixed population of Greeks from across the Hellenistic world, Egyptians, Jews (probably the largest Jewish community in the world) and people of a hundred other nations, including, later in its history, Romans. Its iconography, culture and religions were highly syncretic – for instance, statues in tombs are Egyptian in style but with Roman clothing and hair styles. There are many depictions of the Hellenistic Ptolemies in Egyptian idioms, such as sphinxes bearing their heads. Ancient Egyptian statues, obelisks and other structures were brought to Alexandria from other sites, as with Tanis (see

A late 19th-century conception of the Lighthouse of Pharos. In practice the Lighthouse probably had three tiers. The light itself was said to be produced by a furnace at the top of the tower, and there were also fanciful reports of a giant mirror or lens that helped project the light, and which could be used as a weapon or to magnify distant objects. The Lighthouse was the last of the Seven Wonders, other than the pyramids, to remain standing. Although severely damaged in earthquakes in the 4th century CE, it was repaired and survived many more earthquakes in increasingly ruinous form. The lowest portion survives to this day as part of the Qait Bey Fort.

page 98). Yet for all this, Alexandria was emphatically *not* Egyptian. It was often described as *Alexandria ad Aegyptum*, meaning 'Alexandria-adjoining-Egypt', and in Roman times the local governor bore the title 'Prefect of Alexandria and Egypt'.

Under Ptolemaic and later Roman patronage, Alexandria became the world's greatest city. Its population swiftly grew to number in the hundreds of thousands (according to some estimates it later reached a million). It was the epicentre of trade for the Mediterranean world, well situated to take advantages of the trade routes from the Red Sea and Arabia that linked the Greco-Roman world to the Persian, Indian and Chinese worlds. It had the world's largest library and academic faculty, and its institutions (see below) attracted many of the world's great scholars, including Euclid (of geometry fame), Eratosthenes (who calculated the circumference of the Earth) and Aristarchus (who posited a heliocentric solar system). It was in Alexandria that the Old Testament was first translated into Greek, helping to fix its form thereafter, and where cults like those of Isis and Serapis (see below) were established, to spread later across much of the Classical world.

Highlights of Ancient Alexandria

Perhaps the most famous building in Alexandria was the Lighthouse, built on the eastern tip of the island of Pharos (although deposition on either side of the Heptastadion means that Pharos is now part of the mainland). The Lighthouse was one of the Seven Wonders of the Ancient World, a great tower over 100 metres (328 feet) tall, with a fire and a giant mirror at the top to help guide ships into port. The main port was the Great Harbour to the east, while to the west of the

The Roman theatre, or Odeon, in Alexandria. The bottom tier of seats is granite, but the others are of white marble, probably imported from Italy.

A sphinx from Alexandria. Although they were Greek, the Ptolemies co-opted the motifs and symbols of ancient Egypt to legitimize their rule.

Heptastadion was the Eunostos ('safe return') Harbour. The Great Harbour curved round in a semicircle; at its eastern lip a promontory called Cape Lochias was the location for the Ptolemaic palace complex, and around this the Bruchion, or Royal Quarter, where the Greek population was based, and which occupied the north eastern third of central Alexandria. Here were the most magnificent buildings, including the Museum, a temple to the Muses, which was a sort of ancient academy, hosting a permanent staff of scholars and scribes and

attracting the famous names mentioned above. Next to, or possibly inside, the Museum was the Royal Library, also known as the Great Library of Alexandria (see box on page 117).

To the east of the Royal Quarter was the large Jewish quarter, which ruled itself as a semi-autonomous enclave. In the centre of the harbour were the Navalia, or docks, and behind them the Emporium, or Exchange and the Apostases, or Magazines. Also in this area were two temples – the Timonium, built by Mark Anthony, and the Caesarium – and two obelisks, later known as Cleopatra's Needles and removed to London and New York.

Among the numerous other temples the most notable were temples to Isis and Serapis. Isis was a traditional Egyptian goddess redefined to a much wider role as a sort of Greco-Roman super-goddess, while Serapis was a Ptolemaic invention, a combination of the Egyptian gods Osiris and Apis (the sacred bull god) designed specifically to give Alexandria a patron deity and provide the disparate Greek and Egyptian inhabitants with a common religious focus. The Serapeum, the main temple in Alexandria, was sited on a rocky outcrop in the south of the city, with 100 steps leading up to it. Among other functions, it also served as an auxiliary or 'daughter' library to the main, or Royal Library. West of the Serapeum was located one of Alexandria's many cemeteries, now known as the Catacombs of Kom el Shoqafa, a remarkable confluence of Egyptian custom and style with Greek and Roman influences. This part of town was the Rhakotis Quarter, where the Egyptians lived.

Decline and Fall

Under the Romans Alexandria became the second city in the empire, but it also became increasingly fractious and violent. Tensions between the city's ethnic groups flared up regularly, with pogroms against the Jews, for instance, while Roman emperors such as Caracalla visited destruction and massacres on the city. The ascendancy of

Christianity, which made Alexandria into one of the leading centres of the early Church, simply added to the tensions, culminating in vicious anti-pagan rampages by the patriarch Theophilus in 391 CE, when he led a mob that razed the Serapeum, and his nephew Cyril, who was responsible for the death of the pagan mathematician and philosopher Hypatia in 412 CE. Severe earthquakes also took their toll and the city was much diminished when conquered by the Arabs in 640 CE, although it was still magnificent enough for General Amr ibn al-As to report back to Caliph Omar that the city had '4,000 palaces, 4,000 baths and 400 theatres'.

Changes in trade routes and the establishment of a new capital by the Muslims caused Alexandria to dwindle still further, so that by the 18th century it was only a small town. Earthquakes, subsidence and rising sea levels meant that most of the Royal Quarter had slipped beneath the waves and only since the mid-1990s has underwater archaeology started to rediscover its remains. For the Georgian sightseer on his Grand Tour, Alexandria was a tremendous disappointment. James Bruce reported in 1768 that 'now we can say of [Alexandria], as of Carthage, *periere ruinae*. Even its ruins have disappeared'.

THE LIBRARY OF ALEXANDRIA

The library has become a legendary place, famed for being almost an order of magnitude larger than any other ancient library, while its destruction has become the archetype of cultural vandalism, described as 'the day that history lost its memory'. It was said to host more than 500,000 books, a vast collection built up by Ptolemaic edicts requiring every visitor to Alexandria to surrender any scrolls in their possession for copying, by the wholesale larceny of the library of Athens and by the annexation of the collection of the rival library at Pergamum (transferred to Alexandria as a gift to Cleopatra by her lover Mark Anthony). In practice, however, the Great Library's size has probably been exaggerated – a building that could hold this many books would have needed some 40 kilometres (25 miles) of shelving, but there is no hint in historical descriptions of Alexandria of a building colossal enough to host this. Comparison with other ancient libraries, in conjunction with other clues, suggests a more realistic figure in the tens rather than hundreds of thousands. An

additional source of confusion is that the Great Library is something of a misnomer, for in addition to the Royal Library there was a 'daughter' library at the Serapeum and possibly others in the city.

The destruction of the library has also become shrouded in legend. Several culprits are blamed. Julius Caesar accidentally set fire to a large portion of the city when besieged by a mob in 47 BCE; a Christian mob under Patriarch Theophilus razed pagan temples in 391 CE and Muslim forces that conquered Egypt in 640 CE supposedly burned the books to heat the city's bath-houses, on the basis that any scrolls that contradicted the Koran were heretical and any that agreed with it were superfluous. This last story is almost certainly a myth, but it is possible that the other two culprits do share some blame. It is also the case that Alexandria suffered numerous other insults, with a number of Roman emperors visiting death and destruction on the city in response to rebellions or perceived slights. Most likely there was not a single destructive event, but several, culminating in the ruin of the Serapeum.

LEPTIS MAGNA

LOCATION: LIBYA
DATE OF CONSTRUCTION: 1000 BCE
ABANDONED: c 6TH CENTURY CE
BUILT BY: PHOENICIANS; ROMANS
KEY FEATURES: ARCH OF SEVERUS; ARCH OF TRAJAN;
AMPHITHEATRE; CIRCUS; THEATRE; VILLAS AND MOSAICS

One of the best preserved of all ancient Roman cities is Leptis Magna (also Lepcis Magna), on the coast of what is now Libya (130 kilometres (81 miles) east of Tripoli). In its heyday it was the third most important city in Africa, after Alexandria and Carthage. The remains of a range of public buildings, particularly of the theatre, amphitheatre and a magnificent arch erected in honour of the city's most famous son, the emperor Septimius Severus, bear testament to the splendour of the city in its heyday. Of particular significance are the discoveries of exquisite mosaics at luxury villas on the outskirts of Leptis, which rank among the greatest Roman works of art ever produced.

While the material fabric of many other ancient cities has been lost because of quarrying by later inhabitants of the area (see Tanis page 100, for example), Leptis Magna largely avoided this fate because until recently there was no significant population centre in its vicinity. In addition, much of the city was constructed from high-quality, erosion-resistant hard limestone, sourced from a nearby quarry that supplied the city from the 1st century BCE until the 2nd century CE (when it became more fashionable to build in marble). Finally, the encroaching dust and sand of this desert region covered up much of the city, preserving it for modern archaeologists to rediscover.

Crossroads by the Sea

Although best known as a Roman city, Leptis Magna long predated the Romans. Initially founded around 1000 BCE as a Phoenician city, possibly on the site of a pre-existing Berber settlement (the Berbers were the indigenous peoples of the region), it later fell within the orbit of Carthage, the trading empire with its own roots in Phoenicia. But Carthage clashed with Rome, suffering catastrophic defeat in the Second Punic War; the victors forced it to restrict its sphere of influence and Leptis increasingly became an independent city. After Carthage's final obliteration in the Third Punic War in 146 BCE, it fell to the Roman client king, Massinissa of Numidia, and then into the orbit of Rome, and was finally formally incorporated into the empire in the reign of Tiberius (14–37 CE).

The Phoenicians had probably chosen to site a colony here because of Wadi Lebda, the seasonal river that reaches the coast at this point that provided a source of water in an otherwise largely arid region and by the site's advantages as a natural harbour protected from storms by offshore islands. Later it would gain greater mercantile/economic significance as a waypoint along the coastal highway that ran from Alexandria through Cyrene to (the refounded Roman colony of) Carthage. As well as trans-African trade, Leptis was a major exporter of grain and olive oil to Rome and a shipping point for the constant stream of exotic animals demanded by the circuses of Rome.

Favourite Son

Under Roman rule Leptis Magna became increasingly prosperous. Local officials and rich citizens paid for major public buildings, like the amphitheatre built in 56 CE or the harbour's northern protective mole, also constructed around the same time. Under the emperor Trajan (98–117 CE), the city was granted *colonia* status, being renamed *Colonia Ulpia Traiana Lepcitanorium*. This conferred major economic and political advantages – for instance, all free-born male inhabitants became full Roman citizens.

Trajan was succeeded by Hadrian, whose taste for marble influenced the subsequent look of the city and under whose governance major new hydrological works were instituted. Wadi Lebda, the main source of water for the city, could be unpredictable and occasionally dangerous when storms brought flash floods and Roman engineers had already constructed overflow channels and dams to help guard against flood damage, together with cisterns and basins for the storage of rainwater. But the growing population of the city, which may have reached 80,000 at its height, together with the demands of agriculture, meant that still more water was needed and a new aqueduct was constructed to bring water overland from Wadi Camm, 19 kilometres (12 miles) away. This additional supply helped to feed the massive new public baths complex – one of the largest outside of Rome – completed in 127 CE.

But the heyday of Leptis Magna was yet to come, for in 193 CE Septimius Severus was acclaimed emperor and went on to rule until 211 CE. Severus had been born in

The monumental tetrapylon Arch of Severus. Note the broken pediments.
Overleaf: The restored Roman theatre. It was originally financed by a wealthy man, Annobal Tapapius Rufus, who had also funded construction of the city's market, the Macellum.

Leptis and came from local stock; he did not forget his roots. He initiated a major programme of public works and in 203 CE he visited the city and exempted it from property and land taxes.

This marked the zenith of Leptis Magna's fortunes, for the stability of Severan rule was soon followed by a succession of weak and divided leaders, with civil war, barbarian invasion and economic turmoil in what is known by historians as the Crisis of the 3rd Century.

International trade collapsed and cities like Leptis bore the brunt. The population declined and by the 4th century the city was weak and vulnerable to Berber raids. Worse was to come, with a massive earthquake in 365 CE levelling many buildings. In 455 CE rampaging Vandals, pillaging their way through North Africa, conquered Leptis and tore down its walls, a move that was to prove short-sighted. The Vandals settled down and established a kingdom based around Carthage, but Leptis had been left vulnerable and was razed in a devastating Berber attack in 523 CE, from which it never recovered.

Eleven years later the Byzantine general Belisarius destroyed the Vandal kingdom, recaptured Leptis and erected new walls, but, as the Byzantine chronicler Procopius records, 'not however on as large a scale as it was formerly, but much smaller, in order that the city might not again be weak because of its very size, and liable to capture by the enemy, and also be exposed to the sand.' Although it was designated the provincial capital, Leptis had suffered too much and by the time of the Arab invasion in the mid-7th century, the city was almost deserted but for its garrison of Byzantine soldiers. The site was entirely abandoned to the encroaching dust and sand until excavations began in modern times.

Rough Guide to Leptis Magna

Only a portion of the site has been excavated, but many impressive ruins still stand, while archaeologists have uncovered clues about other major buildings. The basic plan of the city reflects its old and new parts, both with gridlike street patterns, but with the original Punic city at a slightly different orientation to the later Roman expansion. The main axis of the Roman city was the Cardo Maximus, the main street, which ran from the old market area in the northeast to intersect with the main coast road, just outside the city limits to the southeast. The latter formed the city's Decumanus (the other primary axis, which would normally run through the centre of town).

At the junction of these two main roads is one of the most impressive monuments to be seen in Leptis Magna, the magnificent Arch of Severus. Erected by the citizens to celebrate the accession of one of their own to the imperial purple, the arch is unusual in being a *tetrapylon* or *quadrifrons* – i.e. having four pillars and four arches. Although the current arch is a reconstruction from the 1920s, archaeologists have been able to determine that it was probably adapted from a pre-existing structure built long before the time of Severus and that it seemed to have taken as long as eight years to complete, with work starting, halting and then being rapidly completed in anticipation of his visit to the city in 203 CE.

The decoration of the arch is unusual and in some places of very high quality. There are scenes of defeated enemies, identified from their clothing as Parthians, who Severus had campaigned against successfully at the start of his reign, as well as scenes of the imperial family. The emperor's wife and two sons, Caracalla and Geta, are shown, joining hands with the emperor in a scene representing the spirit of concord (somewhat ironically, given that Caracalla would have his brother murdered and his name officially condemned immediately on assuming power). Other features of the arch are broken pediments (rare) and figures of Victory and local gods, such as Melqart, who the Romans identified with Hercules. Features such as the broken pediments suggest that the arch was designed by someone from the eastern provinces, rather than Rome.

Along the Cardo Maximus to the northeast is the Arch of Trajan. To the left of this, partially cut into a hill, is the city's theatre, the oldest and second largest in Roman Africa, built around 1 or 2 CE. Until the construction of the amphitheatre, it may have been used to stage gladiatorial combats. It features a temple, possibly constructed here to circumvent Roman strictures on theatres as immoral – with a temple on site the building became sacred and could not be torn down. To the southeast of the Cardo is the Severan Basilica, or law courts, which became a church in Byzantine times. At its northeastern end the Cardo led to the Old Forum, the oldest part of town where the original Punic settlement was centred, where many temples were situated. To the east of this was the harbour, including port buildings and even a lighthouse – a smaller replica of the great one at Alexandria (see page 112).

A kilometre to the east of the city lie the amphitheatre and circus. Little is left of the latter, which sat where the beach is today, but in ancient times it could seat up to 25,000 people, who came to watch chariot races and other sports. The amphitheatre, however, is largely intact. With seating for 16,000 people and an oval arena measuring 57 x 47 metres (187 x 154 feet), it was built in the bowl left by a former quarry. Inscriptions reveal that the best seats, favoured by the rich elite of Leptis, were those on the southeastern side, where a breeze from the sea helped to keep spectators cool.

Villas Fit for Princes

Some of the most remarkable finds have come from the surrounding countryside, where rich citizens lived in luxurious villas and displayed their wealth and taste through exquisite mosaics, some of which have survived. In 2000 the best mosaic yet was uncovered by archaeologists from the University of Hamburg, lining the cold plunge pool of the bath-house of a villa to the south of Leptis. The mosaic shows an exhausted gladiator, taking a breather while surveying his defeated opponent. Speaking to *The Times* newspaper, Roman art expert Mark Merrony described it as, 'nothing less than a Roman masterpiece executed by the Sandro Botticelli of his day… I have never seen such a vibrantly realistic depiction of a human [in Roman mosaic art].'

However, controversy erupted over the decision to cut the mosaic out from its site and transplant it to the

A gorgoneion, or Gorgon's head – one of a series along a colonnade at Leptis Magna. Gorgoneions were regarded as good luck charms and protective symbols, helping to ward off ill fortune and the evil eye, perhaps in a kind of magical inversion of the dread power of the Gorgon Medusa, whose gaze turned men into stone.

local museum. Detractors claim that the operation was clumsy and damaged the mosaic, but defenders insist it was the best move and point to wider problems with low levels of funding in Libyan archaeology and heritage. This relates to wider concerns about the increasing impact of tourism on the heretofore little-visited Leptis Magna, which is not being met with increasing standards of stewardship of this ancient Roman treasure trove.

SOUTH ASIA AND THE FAR EAST

Again, this chapter covers a huge swathe of time, featuring cities dating back to the dawn of civilization in South Asia (in the 3rd millennium BCE) and cities that flourished in the Middle Ages, reflecting the breadth of cultures in the region. But despite the differences, there are parallels between cities as widely separated in time and space as Harappa, in the Indus Valley and Fujiwara-kyo in Japan.

Harappa and its sister city Mohenjo-daro were truly lost cities, in the sense that no one knew or remembered that they or the cultures that had given birth to them had ever existed. Locals knew of the great mounds that contained the remnants of the cities, but there was no way for them to know what the mounds represented. Instead they wove folk tales and fairy stories around them, telling of dancing troupes of little people atop the mounds. Only in the 20th century did the existence become apparent of a major centre of early civilization to rank alongside Mesopotamia or ancient Egypt.

By contrast, Fujiwara-kyo was a comparative latecomer to the world stage, founded some 3,500 years after Harappa. But like the Indus Valley city, it represented its region's first experiment in urbanism, for it was the first genuine city to be constructed in Japan.

Angkor, in Cambodia, grew more organically, but came to outdo in magnificence and size any city in the Far East. While it is historically much closer to the modern era, it is in some ways more strange and different from modern expectations of a city than the much more ancient Indus Valley cities. The modern city-dweller can recognize and relate to the blocks of multi-storey brick buildings and the canyon-like streets of Harappa, but Angkor seems not to be a city at all, for there appears to be no sign of common dwellings or even of palaces or government buildings. All that is left is a collection of temples.

Smiling faces look out to the cardinal points from the towers of the Buddhist Bayon Temple in Angkor Thom, part of the Khmer city of Angkor. Modern Khmer call these faces Prohm Bayon.

HARAPPA

LOCATION: INDUS VALLEY, PAKISTAN

DATE OF CONSTRUCTION: *c* 2800 BCE

ABANDONED: *c* 1500 BCE

BUILT BY: INDUS CIVILIZATION, ALSO KNOWN AS HARAPPANS

KEY FEATURES: MUNICIPAL PLUMBING AND SEWAGE; STREET GRID; BEADS, SEALS, PLAQUES, WEIGHTS, FIGURINES; LACK OF MONUMENTAL OR PUBLIC ART

Harappa and its sister city Mohenjo-daro (see page 130) are two of the largest cities of the Indus civilization (also known as the Harappan civilization), the least known and most mysterious of the four original centres of Old World civilization. While ancient Egypt, Mesopotamia and China are relatively familiar, heavily excavated and researched and, crucially, accessible to us through their own words thanks to their writings and inscriptions, the Indus civilization remains enigmatic, even though it was the largest and in some respects the most sophisticated of the four ancient states. What language did the people of Harappa speak? What does their script record? Who ruled them and how? What gods did they worship? What kind of legacy did they bequeath to the people who now inhabit their ancient territory?

The first Europeans to see the great mounds of the Indus Valley assumed they were relics from the early days of Hindu-Buddhist civilization, the recorded history of which began with the Mauryan Dynasty of 321 BCE. The explorer Charles Masson, for instance, the first European to report the ruins of Harappa after stumbling upon them in the late 1820s, assumed it was the stronghold of King Porus, defeated by Alexander the Great in 326 BCE. In 1875, the first of a series of strange seals engraved with an unknown script was discovered at Harappa, pointing to the possibility that the mound concealed the remains of an entirely new civilization. But it was not until 1924, when the Archaeological Survey of India announced the first results of excavations at Harappa and Mohenjo-daro, that the existence of a previously unknown Bronze Age civilization was conclusively revealed.

By this time the site at Harappa had already suffered catastrophic damage thanks to the depredations of the railway. When the Lahore-Multan railway line through the area had been constructed in the 1850s, workers had used the vast quantities of bricks that peeked through the surface of the great mounds as a ready source of ballast and large areas of the ancient city had been destroyed.

The Indus Civilization

But the damage wrought by brick scavengers has not prevented archaeologists from building a picture of the civilization that was centred on large urban settlements such as Harappa. The roots of the Indus civilization date back as far as 7000 BCE, when villages in the Indus Valley and the adjacent hill country that marks the border between the Indian sub-continent and the Iranian region first developed. In the Chalcolithic Era (or

Courses of brick masonry at Harappa, which demonstrate why 19th-century workers on the railway viewed the ruins as a rich quarry for useful ballast materials.

Copper Age), from about 4300–3200 BCE, these villages grew quite large and spread their influence throughout the Indus Valley region, where the great River Indus and the now extinct River Sarasvati flooded annually, bringing great fertility but also great obstacles to settlement.

From around 3700–2800 BCE villages began to develop along the Ravi River, one of the tributaries of the Indus, and this period saw the spread of a homogenous culture through the region, with toy models of bullock carts attesting to the growth of trade routes, which already reached for hundreds of miles, and specialized craft technologies involving metalwork, pottery and jewellery (that would later be central to the Indus civilization) spreading as well. At this time the region may have had stronger seasonal variation in temperature than now, with the floodplains and surrounding areas providing rich hunting and fishing as well as fertile arable land. Precursors to what would later become a full-blown writing system began to appear, in the form of symbols inscribed onto pottery.

From 2800–2600 BCE Harappa grew into a large town, covering more than 25 hectares (61¾ acres) in two walled zones. Crafts, trade and social organization all became increasingly developed. By 2600 BCE the fully urban Harappan phase (or the Indus civilization) began and for 700 years Harappa dominated the surrounding region. It grew into a huge city of up to 80,000 people (the population probably fluctuated over the year, with market season bringing in hordes of outlying folk) that covered over 150 hectares (370½ acres) with a circumference of more than 5 kilometres (3 miles).

The Indus civilization itself spread its influence over an area the size of Western Europe and twice as large as ancient Mesopotamia or Egypt, with more than 1,500 known settlements centred on what are now the provinces of Punjab and Sindh in Pakistan, and spreading into northwestern states of India as far as the Ganges Valley, southwest into what is now Kutch and Gujarat, and

west as far as northern Afghanistan. Materials found in Harappa attest to a trade network that stretched from Central Asia to Mesopotamia and Arabia, with raw materials imported to the city where artisans produced manufactured goods for export – for example, decorated carnelian beads from the workshops of the Indus civilization have been found at sites in Mesopotamia and Persia.

The Harappans also developed sophisticated systems for regulating trade, ownership and transactions. Seals with standardized symbols and a form of hieroglyphic writing known as the 'Indus script' were widespread, and it is thought they were probably used to mark goods with quantities and ownership. Similarly marked copper plaques may have been the start of a system of currency, while small tokens of faience and fired steatite (also known as soapstone) inscribed with marks may have been used for accounting purposes. Tablets of clay or faience (see below) have been found snapped in half, and they may have been used to regulate contracts, with each party to a transaction retaining half of the tablet until it was completed. A common class of find at Harappa is small stone cubes of graduated sizes. These were standardized weights used to ensure fair transactions in the trade of high value merchandise, such as jewellery.

Sophisticated, Structured City

One of the best-known features of the Indus civilization was its highly advanced urban planning and sewerage system. Harappa featured a water infrastructure of a scale and sophistication not seen anywhere else until Roman times, and even then only in the richest areas of a city, whereas at Harappa the provisions were universal. Numerous brick-lined wells scattered around the city provided a steady supply of water, while houses were equipped with bathrooms and latrines, which emptied into sewage drains, themselves connected to municipal main sewers. The sewage was fed to collection points outside the residential zones and was probably carted off to be used as fertilizer for the market gardens surrounding the city.

The same careful planning that is evident in the sewage systems operated on a larger scale; the Indus settlements are remarkable for being the world's first planned cities. Mesopotamian and Egyptian cities grew organically, with no strategic planning resulting in winding streets, warrens of lanes and alleys and irregular-shaped buildings. By contrast, Harappa was laid out on a grid system not seen again until the Greek cities of the mid-1st millennium BCE, with wide central avenues, regular shaped buildings and the aforementioned water infrastructure built into the fabric of the city. The street grid was oriented to the cardinal points of the compass and the major avenues were more than 8 metres (26¼ feet) wide. Along some of them were central dividers suggesting a two-lane system for regulating bullock-cart traffic.

Harappa comprised three main walled areas (that left three large mounds for archaeologists to pick over) and surrounding walled suburbs. Massive walls of mud brick, with brick gateways, served multiples purposes: control of access into the city, defence and also protection from floods. Evidence of military might and associated socio-political power structures is noticeably absent from Harappa and the other cities, with no monumental art or reliefs, no depictions of proud emperors or conquering armies. It is hard to identify any remaining buildings as palaces or temples, although one of the main zones of Harappa is described as a 'citadel', and each walled area probably had some public/administrative/religious function. The absence of the normal signs of authority (i.e. of a king or emperor) is part of the wider enigma concerning the Indus civilization. How did it come to control such a wide area and how was it governed? Who was in charge? It is thought likely that government was by a sort of corporate model rather than a centralized monarchy, with each city ruled by its own elite class, who possibly combined religious and secular authority.

Beads

Harappan arts and crafts encompassed pottery, small statues, gold and silver jewellery, bronze tools and seals and tokens. Almost all of the seals and tokens were marked with the Indus script and sometimes also with animal motifs. These might have had religious connotations, perhaps as totem animals for different tribal groupings or they may have symbolized different classes or clans. The most commonly represented animal was the unicorn, which might have been the symbol for a merchant or trader, but the variety of other animals represented, including elephants, bison, tigers and rhinoceroses, bears testament to the ecological diversity of the region in ancient, probably wetter, times.

Perhaps the most distinctive products of the Indus civilization were beads. Excavations at Harappa show stone beads from every level of occupation and the production of finely wrought and often extremely difficult to make beads from rare and valuable material is one of the defining technologies of the civilization. Figurines from the city show that people wore multiple strings of beads and there may have been a sophisticated 'language' of bead jewellery signalling social status, wealth, power and other attributes. They were also an export commodity. The most common material was steatite, a soft white stone also known as soapstone, but other materials included bronze, carnelian, agate and jasper. The harder the material and the smaller the bead, the more difficult it was to make and excavations at Harappa suggest that different workshops in the city, perhaps under the direction of wealthy patrons, competed to advance their skills. Harappans also developed technologies for glazing and colouring beads, including the technology of faience, where a ceramic or stone is glazed with a lustrous sheen, particularly to make it look like lapis lazuli or turquoise, precious materials that stained easily when worn next to the skin. Later Harappans developed glass beads c 1700 BCE, 200 years before the Egyptians first made glass.

MOHENJO-DARO

LOCATION: INDUS VALLEY, PAKISTAN

DATE OF CONSTRUCTION: *c* 2600 BCE

ABANDONED: *c* 1500 BCE

BUILT BY: INDUS CIVILIZATION, ALSO KNOWN AS HARAPPANS

KEY FEATURES: CITADEL; LOWER TOWN; PLUMBING AND SEWAGE; GREAT BATH; GREAT HALL; ASSEMBLY HALL; STREET GRID; BEADS; SEALS; PLAQUES; WEIGHTS; FIGURINES; LACK OF MONUMENTAL OR PUBLIC ART

The largest and best known of the cities of the Indus civilization is Mohenjo-daro, which, unlike Harappa (see page 126), was spared the depredations of brick-looters and survived beneath its mounds until the 20th century, when wholesale excavation revealed an almost intact brick-built metropolis with lanes and streets sandwiched between towering walls. Having survived 4,500 years, however, the remains of the great city are now under severe threat of crumbling into dust.

On the banks of the Indus, about 402 kilometres (250 miles) upstream from the ocean in the Sindh state of Pakistan, lie the remains of Mohenjo-daro (one of several alternative translations applied is 'Mound of the Dead'). Although the earliest detected period of occupation at the site dates back to 3500 BCE, the main phase of occupation began in 2600 BCE and lasted for another 700 years, during which time the city dominated the southern Indus plain. The total area of the site is over 250 hectares (617 acres), but the heart of the city is split into a Citadel and an adjoining 80-hectare (198-acre) Lower Town, a pattern seen in many of the larger Indus Valley settlements. Almost all of the city is made of kiln-fired bricks, manufactured in huge quantities to standardized dimensions with the ratio 1:2:4.

Today the great mounds left by the city rise up to 12 metres (39¼ feet) above the surrounding flood plain; in ancient times they would have stood even higher. Where today the Indus flows to the east of the city, threatening at times to wash chunks of it away, in ancient times it flowed to the west and the city was strategically positioned between it and the Saraswati, another great river to the east, which has since become extinct.

Citadel and Lower Town

Of the two main areas, the large western mound proved to conceal what is now called the Citadel (or the Acropolis), which was built up over hundreds of years, with mud brick platforms for houses and surrounding city walls that have now eroded away.

Several major buildings have been excavated in the Citadel. Their exact roles are unclear – presumably they were public buildings but were they religious, royal or corporate? A large colonnaded building contains a specially engineered tank or pool, 12 metres (39¼ feet) long, 7 metres (23 feet) wide and up to 2.4 metres (7¾ feet) deep, known as the Great Bath. It was lined with bitumen to waterproof it and was designed to be easy to empty and clean. It is speculated that it might have been for ritual cleansing.

Next to it is a massive structure with narrow hypocaust-like passages in its floor, which led to it being initially identified as a hammam or hot-air bath. Later it was interpreted as the State Granary, where the grain tribute was stored (dispensation of which would have been a key element in exercising authority), on the basis that the passages were ventilation shafts. But the way in which the building was originally excavated means that there is no concrete evidence for this attribution and the more conservative label is probably simply the Great Hall. Other major buildings have been labelled the Assembly Hall and the College or Seminary, on the basis that it was the priest's quarters.

A collection of slightly smaller mounds to the east comprises the Lower Town. Each mound may have represented a walled neighbourhood (although as at Harappa the walls are more likely to have been for control of access or flood defences than fortifications). Gridlike streets are oriented to the cardinal directions, with main avenues up to 10 metres (33 feet) wide and smaller streets separating city blocks that measure around 370 x 250 metres (404½ x 273½ yards) each. Over 700 wells may have supplied the city with water, while each house had bathing areas that fed into covered drains that ran beneath the streets. The wells were so well constructed that they remain intact to this day. Houses generally had at least two storeys and were designed to minimize dust and noise from the crowded streets.

The original scholarly interpretation of the Citadel-Lower Town divide was that the different mounds represented distinct functional sectors: the Citadel was the administrative sector, while the eastern mounds were industrial and residential. It is now thought that these functions shifted between districts over time and that all the areas show evidence of residential and industrial uses at different periods, perhaps representing shifting prosperity or jockeying for political power between districts.

Another Brick in the Wall

Archaeologists and historians have traditionally been rather sniffy about the aesthetics and by extension the culture and spirit of the Indus civilization, as represented by Mohenjo-daro. As at Harappa, no public or large-scale art has been found here; nothing proclaiming military might, imperial glory or even simply urban exuberance. No murals, reliefs, mosaics or monumental sculptures. Almost all of the arts and crafts objects that have been recovered are small – e.g. beads, votive figurines, clay and steatite seals and tablets. The symbols, motifs and styles represented are remarkably homogenous across all the Indus civilization sites, prompting scholars to dismiss the culture of this ancient society as displaying 'a dead level of bourgeois mediocrity'. Confronted with the monotony of Mohenjo-daro's endless brick vistas, which leave the impression of a giant termite mound now bereft of its teeming life, it is hard to disagree.

But there are intriguing suggestions from arts and crafts recovered at Mohenjo-daro that the exuberance of later Hindu/Buddhist aesthetics has its roots in its ancient precursor society. The most famous Indus Valley artefact, a steatite bust of a bearded figure wearing a diadem, usually interpreted as a priest-king, displays a zenlike serenity, while a common figure seen on seals and tablets is of a seated male in a lotus-like yogic position. Also, archaeologists working on Indus sites in Pakistan today draw parallels between modern-day *sang* festivals (annual spring fairs) and the fairs that their excavations show probably visited the same sites, and that were celebrated in the same way, 4,500 years ago.

Overleaf: The Great Bath at Mohenjo-daro. Unlike its sister city Harappa, Mohenjo-daro escaped the attention of the railway workers, and its structures survived in a far better condition. The round building in the background is the Buddhist stupa built atop the mound of Mohenjo-daro in the Kushan era (c 100-250 CE).

The Decline of Mohenjo-daro

The traditional view was that Mohenjo-daro and other cities were abandoned in around 1750–1500 BCE, as the culmination of a general decline of the Indus civilization finished off by the Aryan invasion – the influx of Indo-European peoples recorded in the ancient *Rig Veda*, which tells of the god Indra helping his people to overcome mighty forts and ancient castles. The discovery of a few groups of skeletons at Mohenjo-daro, some with apparent signs of violence and some in attitudes suggesting an escape attempt, lent weight to this attempt to link the ancient Vedic accounts with modern-day archaeological finds, just as Schliemann tried to do for Homer and Troy (see page 40).

Today there is considerable doubt over whether there ever was an Indo-Aryan 'invasion', and a more considered view of the archaeological record shows that occupation continued at Mohenjo-daro and other sites long beyond 1500 BCE. There are gaps in the archaeological record but it is considered unlikely that the city was ever fully abandoned due to its favourable position high above the floods.

But Mohenjo-daro did undoubtedly decline and dwindle. During the late phase of occupation, from 1900 BCE on, there is evidence that the city became increasingly crowded, with rooms subdivided and streets encroached upon, and that social order and central control were breaking down, leaving drains

This steatite statue, known as the Priest-King, is the most famous artefact of the Indus Valley Civilization. The diadem and the eyes may have originally been inlaid, while small holes beneath the ears suggest that a necklace would have been attached. The cloak he wears is decorated with trefoil patterns, which were originally filled with red pigment. The back of the head is flat and may have had another piece attached, representing a bun or headdress.

unrepaired and city walls unmaintained. Cuboid weights, inscribed seals and tablets, distinctive pottery marked with Indus script and raw materials and trade goods from far away – all the indicators of a functioning, well-ordered culture – disappear. Mentions in Mesopotamian texts of trade with Meluhha, a nation generally accepted to be the Indus civilization, cease.

There were probably multiple causes for this decline. As mentioned above, there were major changes to the Indus and Sarasvati rivers. The latter dried up altogether, presumably driving large numbers of people who had depended on it to seek aid and sustenance elsewhere, contributing to overcrowding in Mohenjo-daro. Meanwhile the Indus changed course, damaging the city and disrupting its agricultural base. Possibly these riverine changes were linked to wider ecological problems – the industrial-scale brick production of Indus Valley cities, together with their other industries, must have consumed vast quantities of wood, which in turn could have led to deforestation and consequent climate changes (lower rainfall, flash floods, etc.).

With the decline of the Indus civilization the archaeological record shows the spreading influence of new cultures that represents a restructuring of the overall social order. Some of these cultural traditions are indigenous to the northwestern subcontinent and others indicate connections to the northwest and to the east. Eventually a new social order emerged in which new technologies were dominant – use of the horse, use of iron, and also new languages and religion that can be linked to Vedic and early Hindu, Jain and Buddhist culture.

What became of the Indus Valley people? According to Jonathan Mark Kenoyer, the leading authority on Indus civilizations, most of them probably stayed put and blended with the new cultural arrivals. This contrasts with the popular view of what happens when

MOHENJO-DARO IN PERIL

Tragically, having lasted intact for so many millennia, Mohenjo-daro is currently at severe risk. Exposure to the elements, floodwaters from the Indus and most of all poorly controlled salinity in the soils of the region, exacerbated by wasteful irrigation techniques, threaten to eat away at the bricks of the ancient city. Some of the oldest excavated areas have already crumbled into dust. Pakistani and UNESCO supported projects have spent millions of dollars on conservation and research, but so far have not been successful in preserving the city. The solution long proposed by archaeologists has been to rebury most of the city and only leave a small area exposed for tourists. At present, the Department of Archaeology, Government of Pakistan has experimented with partial reburial and intensive conservation that has seen some positive results. Future plans include extensive coring and subsurface survey of the surrounding area to find the true limits of the site, followed by selective excavations to better understand the chronology of the settlement.

In the course of new excavations at Mohenjo-daro and Harappa, as well as the many sites being excavated in other regions of Pakistan and India, it is possible that many mysteries of this civilization will gradually be revealed.

a new civilization takes over an area – for instance, the Aryan Invasion – which generally envisages wholesale population replacement. In practice genetic studies show that while the cultures may change, populations are remarkably invariant; in other words, the roles may be different, but the actors stay the same.

ANGKOR

LOCATION: CAMBODIA

DATE OF CONSTRUCTION: 802 CE

ABANDONED: LARGELY ABANDONED BY 1431 CE

BUILT BY: KHMER EMPIRE

KEY FEATURES: ANGKOR WAT; ANGKOR THOM; BAYON TEMPLE; *BARAY* (RESERVOIRS); LACK OF NON-SACRED BUILDINGS

The great legacy of the Khmer Empire and arguably the greatest religious complex of all time, the city of Angkor is a remarkable collection of temples and canals, buried under thick jungle when it was first encountered by European explorers. Recent hi-tech investigations have revealed its full, colossal extent and provided valuable clues about the self-inflicted environmental problems that may have caused its demise, but the authorities seem powerless to prevent the continual degradation of the ancient treasure by looters.

Angkor is a Khmer word derived from the Sanskrit term for 'holy city'. It was the capital and religious centre of the Khmer Empire, a state that flourished in Indochina from the 9th to the 15th centuries CE. West of the Mekong River, near Tonle Sap – the largest lake in Indochina – on a wide, low-lying plain in the centre of modern-day Cambodia, Angkor grew over the centuries into the largest – in geographical terms – pre-industrial city in history, with a population that may have numbered as many as a million. But to the modern visitor there is little that resembles a city; instead there is a collection of temples and water features widely scattered around a scrubby plain interrupted by patches of thick jungle. How could this strange landscape have supported such a vast population and what could have motivated the construction of such a profusion of religious architecture?

Seat of the Khmer God-kings

The region of Indochina known today as Cambodia was a collection of small states known to its northern neighbours, the Chinese, as Zhenla. At the start of the 9th century CE the Khmer king Jayavarman II, ruler of Kambuja, united the fragmented principalities of the region and extended his sway over most of Indochina. In 802 CE he declared himself to be *devajara*, meaning 'royal god' – effectively labelling himself as 'god-king' and establishing the royal personality cult as the central strategy by which the monarchy legitimized its rule – a strategy that was to lead to the incredible sacred architecture of Angkor.

In 889 CE Yasovarman I moved the capital of the Khmer Empire to Angkor and set about transforming it into a sacred landscape: a replica of heaven on Earth. In the mythology of Hinduism, the state religion of the Khmers, the centre of heaven was Mount Meru, the abode of the gods, which was surrounded by the oceans. On Phnom Bakheng, the only natural hill in the area, Yasovarman built a pyramidal temple, symbolizing and recreating Mount Meru. Within the temple a sacred stone, or *lingam*, represented Shiva, one of the supreme Hindu gods but also the Khmer god-king. Thus the Khmer god-kings gave physical expression to their divine right to rule, legitimizing their authority through the very fabric of their capital.

To complete the earthly reconstruction of the cosmology, the temple at Phnom Bakheng was surrounded by a moat, to represent the oceans, and this was fed from the first of two huge reservoirs, or *baray*, constructed at the site. The Eastern Baray at Angkor is 7.5 x 1.8 kilometres (5 x 1 miles) in area and held up to 37 million cubic metres (48,400,000 cubic yards) of water; the Western Baray is even larger. They were the largest manifestation of the massive and complex system of irrigation channels, canals, moats and ponds – over a thousand of them – that underpinned life in Angkor. With this network of water-management features the Khmer were able to tame the annual flooding of Tonle Sap, irrigating their rice paddies and making their agriculture highly productive. A 13th-century Chinese visitor to Angkor (see below), recorded that they could produce three or four crops of rice a year, making it possible to support a huge population spread across a vast urban sprawl. Between 1992 and 2007, researchers using satellites, NASA radar imagery, light aircraft and more down-to-earth technology such as scooters, were able to show that at its height Angkor had covered 1,000 square kilometres (386 square miles), making it the largest pre-industrial city in history. The next biggest rival, the Mayan city of Tikal (see page 170) was more than an order of magnitude smaller at 100–150 square kilometres (38½–58 square miles).

Angkor's glory years came in the 11th to 13th centuries. Under King Suryavarman I (reigned 1011–1050), the imperial palace-city of Angkor Thom began to take shape as a sort of capital within the capital. Suryavarman II (reigned 1113–1150) built Angkor Wat, the most

Bas relief from Angkor Wat showing dancing asparas – female spirits or divinities also known as sky-dancers or celestial dancers.
Overleaf: The colossal temple of Angkor Wat, viewed from across the wide moat that surrounds it. The moat symbolizes the oceans, and the towers the peaks of sacred Mount Meru.

famous and the greatest of the temples at Angkor, intended as his mausoleum. According to an inscription in the temple, Suryavarman II won the throne after slaying a

rival prince in battle, leaping onto his war-elephant and engaging him in single combat. Like the earlier temples, Angkor Wat with its five towers was a version of the sacred Mount Meru, which according to the myth had five peaks.

The greatest of the Khmer kings and the last great builder at Angkor was Jayavarman VII (reigned 1181–1220), who refurbished Angkor Thom, built temples to his parents, and, on adopting Mahayana Buddhism as his personal faith, constructed the Buddhist temple of Bayon in the heart of Angkor Thom. It is famous for the giant faces peering out from its towers, representing King Jayavarman VII as the bodhisattva Avalokiteshvara: thus the king contrived to maintain and even enhance the cult of royal personality despite the change in religion.

The Record of Zhou Daguan

In 1296 a Chinese diplomat, Zhou Daguan, visited Kambuja and wrote an account of life in Angkor, *A Record of the Customs of Cambodia*, which provides an invaluable record of the medieval kingdom. He described the main temples and also depicted a society governed both by pervasive religious devotion and the strict and oppressive hierarchies that fed off that devotion to maintain their status and prerogatives. The elite emphasized the importance of subordination and owned hundreds of slaves who were often treated very poorly.

Yet in some ways life in Kambuja was easier than in China, with the result that there was a significant population of Chinese ex-pats who had fled their homeland. The first thing that such a new arrival had to do, Zhou Daguan reported, was obtain a wife, because trade was an exclusively female preserve. He also described the typical domestic set-up, offering a valuable clue to the mystery of why, beyond infrastructure such as canals and bridges, there seems to be little trace of the non-religious aspect of this heavily populated city. The typical Kambujan home was apparently devoid of furniture and many of the implements and utensils they used were 'disposable' – for

instance, 'they use a tree leaf to make a little bowl and jiao leaves to make a little spoon to take the broth to their mouths. When they have finished using these things they throw them away.' (Similar bowls are still used in parts of Cambodia today.)

Applied on a larger scale, this principle of using natural materials might explain why only the religious monuments are left. Building in stone was reserved for the residences of the gods; apart from infrastructure, secular buildings, apparently up to and including royal palaces, were made from timber or even more perishable materials, which did not long survive the abandonment of the city thanks to the tropical climate.

The Loss and Rediscovery of Angkor

After Jayavarman VII's death there was a brief return to Hinduism, which saw widespread defacing and desecration of Buddhist imagery, but eventually Buddhism was established as the state religion of the Khmers and many of the temples were converted to Buddhist shrines. But there was also a general decline in the Khmer Empire (see below) and from the late 13th century it was threatened by the growing power of the Thai (or Siamese) kingdom to the west. According to the popular history of the site, the end of Angkor came in 1431, when the Thai invaded the western provinces of Kambuja and sacked the city, at which point the Khmer fled to the new Khmer capital near Phnom Penh, taking their treasures with them. In practice, historians have largely discredited this story, and substantial populations continued into the 16th century, possibly as lay support for communities of Buddhist monks based in the temples. But the centre of political gravity had shifted irrevocably and Angkor subsided until it was a shadow of its former glories. By the 17th century, the population had diminished substantially, and in the tropical heat and humidity the jungle quickly reclaimed the site and the roots of fig trees and other plants wreaked considerable damage on the unmortared masonry, forcing blocks apart and threatening to bring the mighty temples low.

The extraordinary ruins of Angkor first became famous in Europe thanks to the writings and sketches of French explorer Henri Mahout, who visited the site in 1860. His account vividly depicts the impact of coming upon the cyclopean ruins draped in verdant growth, a sight 'which presents itself to the eye of the traveller, making him forget all the fatigues of his journey, filling him with admiration and delight, such as would be experienced on finding a verdant oasis in the sandy desert'.

In practice, however, Mahout was far from the first European to visit Angkor, which was reported by the Portuguese in 1550. But it was his account that catapulted Angkor to fame as an archetypal lost city, although the wonder and awe it provoked was not limited to Europeans. When Mahout asked the local people who had constructed such marvels they told him it had been built by gods or giants, while Siamese scribes, writing just two centuries after the fall of the Khmer empire, recorded that it was said that 'angels from heaven came to help in building this magnificent city'.

The Mysterious Decline

Since serious scholarship into Angkor began, and particularly since the institution of the École Française d'Extrême-Orient in 1898, there has been much debate over the causes of Angkor's decline. While accounts of the fatal Thai raid of 1431 may be inaccurate, it is generally accepted that Angkor was in terminal decline by the 15th century and there are competing theories about why. One line of argument is that the Khmer regime was exhausted both by continual warfare with its neighbours and by the tremendous demands of the monumental labour that had created Angkor's sacred landscape. King Jayavarman VII, for instance, is renowned as the greatest of the Khmer kings, but for his subjects his mania for construction must have been incredibly taxing.

Towards the end of the Khmer era the state religion became Theravada Buddhism and George Coedès, perhaps the foremost scholar of Angkor, argues that this form of the religion, with its emphasis on the denial of the reality of the individual, was not compatible with the cult of royal personality. Coedès argues that the combination of this with the military and economic exhaustion of the state resulted in an erosion of central authority, which in turn led to a breakdown of maintenance of the irrigation system, with knock-on effects for the agricultural basis of the city's existence.

More recently the water-management system at Angkor has come in for closer scrutiny as the ultimate rather than merely proximate cause of the city's decline. The recent project to map the full extent of ancient Angkor has led to claims that the city's vast urban sprawl became self-defeating. Mass deforestation to meet the demands of the population and the constant construction projects led to soil erosion, while at the same time the water management system simply became too large for effective management. The result was that the irrigation canals became clogged with silt and ceased to function. Other theories about the city's collapse include climate change, with archaeologists from the University of Sydney pointing to the transition from the medieval warm period to the Little Ice Age as the trigger for the city's water crisis, and disease, with the suggestion that breakdown of the irrigation system led to stagnant water, which in turn led to an explosion of malaria-carrying mosquitoes.

Unfortunately the ancient city's decline continues to this day. Initially the fabric of the city was at risk from the encroaching jungle, but now this threat has been replaced with a human one. Ever since it was uncovered Angkor has attracted the attentions of looters and art thieves, and even today professional teams of looters openly survey parts of the site for statues, façades and reliefs they can rip out and sell on. Rapidly increasing tourism at the site could also pose problems.

FUJIWARA-KYO

LOCATION: ASUKA, JAPAN

DATE OF CONSTRUCTION: 682 CE

ABANDONED: 710 CE

BUILT BY: EMPEROR TENMU AND EMPRESS JITO

KEY FEATURES: STREET GRID; IMPERIAL PALACE; HALLS OF STATE;
IMPERIAL AUDIENCE HALL; SUZAKU-MON (MAIN GATE);
CERAMIC ROOFING; YAKUSHIJI TEMPLE; INSCRIBED WOODEN TABLETS
AND COINS

Japan is renowned as a nation where history and tradition are paramount, yet in some respects it has a relatively short history. Construction at Fujiwara-kyo, effectively Japan's first city, was only begun around 682 CE, while in the same period Japan's rulers introduced several technologies commonly associated with civilization, which seem to have been absent until this point. Despite coming to the party late, however, the builders of Fujiwara-kyo – the City of the Wisteria Plain – produced an impressive and well-planned city dominated by a huge imperial palace complex that included the largest building Japan had ever seen.

The construction of Fujiwara-kyo, also Japan's first permanent capital (although this designation is ironic given that it was occupied for just 16 years before the imperial court and the rest of the city's population were uprooted and transplanted to a new capital), was one of the most significant elements of a profound political, social and cultural transformation. It marked and facilitated the transition of Japan from a disparate group of competing chiefdoms to a nation state and can only be understood when interpreted in this light.

Japan in Transition

Japan emerged relatively late from its prehistoric period and its protohistoric period (see Entremont page 86)

extends up to the founding of Fujiwara-kyo. In the 4th and 5th centuries geo-political control was divided amongst the nobility, who comprised a number of powerful and constantly competing families or clans. Among them was the imperial clan from the Yamato region. By the 7th century, however, most of the core territory of Japan had been consolidated under control of the imperial court (which itself was often controlled by one or more non-imperial clans). The Asuka region had emerged as the locus of this control, but the site of the imperial palace, and therefore the de facto capital of Japan, shifted within this area. This period is now known as the Asuka Era.

As Japan became more centralized, it also developed its links to the mainland, to the sophisticated and dominant cultures of China and Korea. The Asuka Era saw large influxes of immigrants from these areas and the introduction of Buddhism as the state religion, among many other Chinese and Korean cultural influences. At the start of the 7th century the Soga clan controlled power, but in 645 the imperial clan reasserted its own dominance. Under Prince Naka-no-Oe, who later became Emperor Tenji, it followed a twin course of adopting Chinese political and socio-economic models domestically, while pursuing a foreign policy designed to limit Chinese influence. The former strategy was known as the Taika Reform, while the latter involved military adventures in Korea, allying Japanese armies with the Korean kingdom of Baekje, which was engaged in a struggle with the southeastern Korean kingdom of Silla and its Tang Chinese allies.

In 663 the imperial court sent an army of 27,000 troops to Korea to assist Baekje, but their combined forces were defeated at the Battle of Hakusonko, and the Tang-supported Silla took control of the whole peninsula. Many Baekje took refuge in Japan and it was feared that the Tang would retaliate and follow on their heels. Tenji pressed on with the domestic reforms aimed at transforming Japan into a viable, strong nation state, able to defend its borders against aggression from similar entities (i.e. the Chinese). The key reform was the introduction of *ritsuryo*, a system of penal and administrative law copied from China, as the basic legal code of the new nation state. Under *ritsuryo* the entire population was subject to legal control – including taxation – from the centre, with the emperor at the top of the pyramid. Administering this new system required an ever-larger bureaucracy and by the 670s it was clear that the confines of the traditional and impermanent imperial palace were insufficient. Plans were put in motion for a new, permanent capital city, following Chinese models. For the first time in Japan, a large settlement would be planned in advance and laid out accordingly.

Short-lived Capital

Construction of the city was begun during the reign of the Emperor Tenmu. A site in the Asuka region was chosen – a plain between three hills in the present day Takadono district of Kashihara-shi, where three of Japan's main roads converged: the Nakatsumichi, Shimotsumichi and Yoko-oji, which were to mark the east, west and north boundaries of the city, respectively. The location had originally been known as Fujiigahara, or 'plain of the wisteria well', but later this was shortened to simply Fujiwara, 'wisteria plain' and so the city became Fujiwara-kyo, 'city of the wisteria plain'. Canals were dug to allow timber and stone to be brought to the site (although these were later filled in before the city was actually occupied).

Tenmu's death in 687 brought a temporary halt to construction, but the project was continued under his widow, the Empress Jito, and finally completed in 694, whereupon Fujiwara-kyo served as her capital. A poem composed by Prince Shiki records some of the emotions stirred by the move to the new city: 'Asuka breezes that once curled back the palace maidens' sleeves; seeing now the court so far, they blow without purpose.'

Fujiwara-kyo was the capital of Jito's successors, the Emperor Mommu and the Empress Gemmei, but in 710 the capital was relocated 14.5 kilometres (9 miles) north, to Nara. Fujiwara-kyo was stripped of all recyclable materials and what remained may have been further devastated by a fire in 711. By the 9th century the site had largely returned to farmland and it was not definitively rediscovered until excavations began in 1934.

Chinese Model City

The city was laid out according to the *jobo* grid system, like a Go board, along the lines of Chinese cities like the Tang capital of Changan. Although it could not compete with Chinese metropolises for size, recent excavations have revealed that it may have covered as much as 25 square kilometres (9¾ square miles), considerably bigger than traditionally believed. The city was divided by orthogonal *oji*, or avenues, into twelve *jo* (north-south blocks) and eight *bo* (east-west blocks). It was at Fujiwara-kyo that the Japanese custom began of dividing the capital into a *sakyo* ('left capital') and *ukyo* ('right capital') along a north-south dividing line. Whereas in later capitals the city blocks were delineated by numbers, at Fujiwara-kyo each block had its own name – e.g. Ohari-machi and Hayashi-mach.

As many as 30,000 people may have lived here. One clue to the population comes from a document called the *Shoku Nihongi*, which records that in 704, 1,505 households in Fujiwara-kyo received bolts of cloth. Household registers (known as *koseki*) from the era – a device introduced as part of the *ritsuryo* system to help keep track of tax payers – show that each household numbered on average more than 16 people, suggesting a minimum population for the city of at least 24,000.

The focal point of the city was the Fujiwara-no-miya, the imperial palace. Like a Chinese palace this was actually a compound or complex of walls, plazas and buildings. Sited in the central north zone of the city, so that the monarch could symbolically look south to survey his dominions, the palace was approximately 1 square kilometre (⅓ square mile) and was surrounded by a 5-metre (16½-feet) wide outer ditch, wooden walls about 5 metres (16½ feet) high and then another, inner ditch. There were three main gates; the main one, the Suzaku-mon, was in the south wall. It led to the heart of the complex: the Dairi, the emperor's personal residence and the Chodoin, the Halls of State, of which the most important was the Daigokuden, the Imperial Audience Hall. At 45 metres (147½ feet) wide, 21 metres (69 feet) deep and 25 metres (82 feet) high, this was the largest building in Japan. The *omiya dodan*, or 'earth platform of the great palace' upon which the Daigokuden rested, still rises above the surrounding plain at the site. Significantly the Audience Hall and other palace buildings were the first in Japan to be roofed with ceramic tiles – another innovation from China. It is estimated that up to two million tiles were used on the palace. Also as in China, public buildings were sited in the midst of wide plazas to enhance their impact on the sovereign's subjects.

Around the palace were the mansions of aristocrats and high-ranking officials. One such mansion near the Suzaku-mon covered 12,000 square metres (129,166 square feet). Lesser bureaucrats and commoners lived further out. There were also several Buddhist temples in the city. One of them, Yakushiji, still exists, having been moved along with the capital to the new site at Nara, where it still stands today (although most of it has been reconstructed at one point or another).

Just as the city itself was an innovation, so its construction and habitation involved other innovations. Fujiwara-kyo saw the first latrines yet found in Japan. Analysis of their contents shows that the inhabitants ate raw vegetables and undercooked fish, such as carp and trout, which gave them worms. To help regulate and facilitate trade, the city also saw the first coins ever minted in Japan. In 1999, archaeologists found a cache of Fuhonsen coins, named for the two *kanji* characters on the front – *fu* and *hon*, meaning 'wealth' and 'basis', thought to be a reference to a legendary Chinese epigram, 'the basis for wealth of the people is food and money'. These coins, dating from the late 7th century and predating the previous earliest known Japanese coins of 708, are thought to represent another stage in the Taika Reform project to modernize Japan, transforming it into a nation state along Chinese lines. It is even suggested that the coins were specifically designed to help educate the public about how to use money.

Another innovation from this period was the use of *mokkan*, inscribed wooden tablets or batons used to help administer the *ritsuryo* system. They could be used as luggage or goods labels, as tallies to help keep track of taxes or as official documents. Over 7,000 have been discovered at Fujiwara-kyo, providing valuable insights into the business of government at this crucial period in Japanese history.

Moving Time

After expending so much time and effort to create a city from scratch, why abandon it after such a short time? The relocation was probably down to political/

symbolic reasons, with the new capital intended to provide an even larger and more impressive backdrop to the new system of government, one which was not associated with the traditional ruling region of Asuka (Nara was slightly further to the north). But historian Hisashi Kano suggests that geomancy – landscape magic – may have played a part in the decision, with the hill directly to the south of Fujiwara-kyo effectively disrupting the feng-shui of the palace. Rather than

The remains of Itabuki-no-miya, the palace of the Emperor Kogyoku, in Asuka province. It was here that in 645 the powerful leader Soga no Iruka was assassinated by the Imperial Clan, marking the beginning of the Taika Reforms. The floor plan shows how pre-Fujiwara palaces were much smaller.

the emperor overlooking his domain from the palace, the hill meant that his palace was itself overlooked.

THE AMERICAS

In the Americas lie perhaps the archetypal lost cities: temples, palaces and pyramids that rear up out of virgin jungle, with only weird petroglyphs to hint at the nature of the cultures that once dwelt there and the dark histories that played out against such awe-inspiring backdrops. Cities such as those of the Maya and the Inca, where a combination of circumstances – the swift and total destruction of indigenous civilizations and cultures, the remoteness of the sites and the rate at which the rainforest encroaches – conspired to allow them to disappear from human ken, remained hidden for hundreds of years. The tales of their rediscovery are equally the stuff of romantic legend, with intrepid explorers hacking through the jungle in search of lost cities of gold.

Other pre-Columbian civilizations left their mark on the Americas, from the mound builders of Mississippi and the canyon-dwelling Pueblo peoples of the southern deserts to the Aztec Empire of Mexico and the mysterious ancient Tiwanaku culture of the Andes. In many cases the remains left by these kingdoms and empires are relatively young, compared to the ancient sites of the Old World, and are therefore in good enough repair to amaze and enthral visitors even today.

From the point of view of the historian, New World civilizations offer a unique opportunity. Unlike in the Old World, where civilizations inevitably developed in the context of a network of influences and legacies that stitch one to another, the New World civilizations developed in glorious isolation, from first principles to fully-formed, sophisticated cultures with writing, monumental masonry and many other forms of technology. The similarities and differences between these lost cities and those of the Old World are instructive and they offer valuable insights into the importance of ecology, the fragility of the environment in the face of urban civilization and the world views of exotic cultures. Perhaps it is this last feature that adds to the allure of the lost cities of the Americas – the religion and mysticism of their builders are both strange and intriguing, lending an extra layer of mystery to the already enigmatic.

El Castillo – 'The Castle' – in Chichen Itza, also known as the Temple of Kukulcan, the Feathered Serpent. Large crowds gather here on the vernal and autumnal equinoxes to watch the sun cast serpentine shadows across the northern face of the pyramid.

CAHOKIA

LOCATION: COLLINSVILLE, ILLINOIS, NR ST LOUIS, MISSOURI, USA
DATE OF CONSTRUCTION: *c* 1050 CE
ABANDONED: *c* 1350 CE
BUILT BY: MISSISSIPPIAN CULTURE
KEY FEATURES: MOUNDS; MONKS MOUND; GRAND PLAZA;
WOODHENGE; PALISADE

In the centre of the American Midwest a collection of manmade mounds mark the site of North America's greatest pre-Columbian city and the centre of a lost civilization ignored by generations of Americans. Huge earthworks and vast landscaped plazas testify to the existence of a well-organized and sophisticated society, but its legacy seems to have vanished almost without a trace.

On the Mississippi floodplains of Illinois, across the river from St Louis, Missouri, lies the World Heritage Site of Cahokia Mounds. This Illinois State Historic Site encompasses some 70 mounds, including the enormous Monks Mound, which has a base larger than that of the Great Pyramid at Giza, but there were originally around 120 in the lost city. The site today covers around 890 hectares (2,200 acres), but in its heyday, around 1100 CE, the city had an area of 1,619 hectares (4,000 acres) and a population that may have numbered as many as 10,000–20,000 people. It was larger than any contemporary city in Europe and not until the 19th century did any city in the New World north of Mexico surpass this.

Cahokia was the apogee of the Mississippian culture (the Cahokian culture), which developed in and around the floodplain known as the American Bottom towards the end of the 1st millennium CE. But because it was pre-literate and collapsed several centuries before the arrival of Europeans, this civilization, and particularly Cahokia

itself, remains shrouded in mystery. It is not known what the inhabitants of the city called it – Cahokia is the name given to the site by local historians who wanted to honour one of the subtribes of the Illiniwek (Illinois) Indians who only arrived in the area in the 1600s – nor is it known who they were or what language they spoke. While it is known that the city appeared almost within a generation, it is not known exactly why this remarkable development occurred nor why it was subsequently abandoned. Were the tribes that lived in the area when the Europeans arrived the descendants of the Mississippians? To what extent can the legacy of this vanished civilization be traced?

Overnight Sensation

The American Bottom offers rich arable land that could be cultivated even without heavy ploughs, and Neolithic peoples there grew crops such as sunflowers and squashes. In the 1st millennium CE the cultivation of corn spread north from Mesoamerica, triggering population growth and the emergence of the formative stages of a recognizable Mississippian culture a little before 1000 CE, evidenced by specific decorative styles on pottery and consistent use of a common set of religious symbols, such as a winged 'bird-man', on pottery, copper and stone artefacts.

The Mississippians lived in villages, but as the population density increased a critical mass was reached until, in

around 1050 CE, the city at Cahokia sprang into existence over a relatively short time, in what some archaeologists have described as a 'big bang' moment. From its centre at Cahokia, Mississippian culture spread its influence over much of the upper Midwest, leaving traces from the present day Canadian border to the Gulf Coast. The adoption of a core set of practices and styles appears to indicate that people all across this area shared a cosmology and related religious system and Cahokia has been described as the Vatican or Mecca of this system.

Cahokia was the ultimate embodiment of the characteristics that mark out the Mississippian culture, including large communal plazas; massive mounds, especially flat-topped ones; wooden palisades; characteristic styles and motifs on pottery etc.; the game of chungke (see below) and the practice of human sacrifice. Although there is evidence of these 'traits' from other Mississippian sites, at Cahokia they were present on a far grander scale than anywhere else.

A reconstruction of the sort of thatched hut that might have housed the majority of Cahokians. Surrounding it is a wooden palisade, a distinctive feature of Mississippian culture.

City of Mounds and Plazas

The most obvious features of Cahokia are the mounds and the Grand Plaza. Mounds at Cahokia came in three main types; each one probably served a different function. Platform or flat-topped mounds, such as Monks, usually had buildings on top of them. Cone-shaped or round-topped mounds were used for burials, while ridge-topped mounds may have served as landmarks or boundary markers, and also appear to have had mortuary functions. The greatest mound – known as Monks Mounds because in 1811 when it was first described by an antiquarian there was a community of Trappist monks living nearby – is over 30 metres (98½ feet) high with a base measuring approximately 300 x 240 metres (984 x 787 feet), one quarter larger than the base of the Great

Pyramid. It has several different terraces and platforms and a flat top where a huge wooden building once sat – possibly the residence of the paramount chief or a temple. Monks Mound was constructed over several centuries, with new material and new layers added periodically, perhaps to mark the death of a leader and the ascension of a new one. It has been estimated that to build it took 15 million baskets of earth deposited over 300 years. The earth came from what are known as borrow pits, some of which are still visible at the site (although many were filled in and even built over).

In 1998 work to install drains on Monks Mound, to help prevent erosion and slippage, led to the discovery of a mysterious layer of stones beneath the western side of the mound. The layer is at least 9.75 metres (32 feet) in extent in one direction, but its full size is unknown and it does not extend under the whole mound. The Mississippians usually preferred to build in earth and wood and the nearest possible source for the stones is at least 12.75 kilometres (8 miles) away, so clearly they must have had some special reason to go to the expense and difficulty of bringing such a mass of stone to the site. Was it a ceremonial platform or structure? Perhaps a tomb or crypt? Was it a repair job or drainage device? The answer must remain a mystery, for the layer is too deep to excavate without removing most of Monks Mound.

Other smaller mounds surround the central Grand Plaza, which at 19 hectares (47 acres) may be the largest earthen city square in the world. It is an artificially flattened area and was skilfully constructed by levelling and filling undulations in the landscape, apparently in a single, vast construction project around 1050 CE, at the birth of Cahokia. An 80-hectare (197½-acre) area comprising the plaza and the mounds around it was enclosed with a 3.25-kilometre (2-mile) long palisade (wall of logs). Although primarily a defensive feature, the stockade also served a ritual function, perhaps marking the boundaries of the sacred precinct. There were smaller plazas elsewhere.

To the west of Monks Mound stood a 'woodhenge' – a circle of cedar posts, used as a solar calculator to determine the timing of equinoxes and solstices. It was rebuilt several times, possibly to take into account the successive enlargements of Monks Mound, the profile of which it was aligned with. This woodhenge suggests that, as with the Mesoamericans, the plazas and pyramids of the Mississippians were part of a solar cult.

The Riddle of Cahokia's Origins

In most civilizations there is a clear progression of intermediate stages of settlement evolution, but Cahokia seems to have emerged and existed as something unique in Mississippian culture, without precedent or antecedent. In practice, however, archaeologists may have found clues regarding formative stages on the path to Cahokia. Groups of mounds to the south of Cahokia, known as the Pulcher and Lohmann Mounds, are thought to be the remnants of much smaller Mississippian settlements/cult centres, and one theory is that these were precursors to Cahokia, where the religious ideas and practices that later triggered the development of the larger city first developed. Elements of the Mississippian culture may also have derived from or been inspired by the Mesoamerican cultures to the south, although no Mesoamerican artefacts have ever been found at Cahokia, indicating that there were no migrations from that region.

Another theory is that Cahokia in effect gave birth to itself. Historian and archaeologist Timothy Pauketat has argued that the abrupt, large-scale coalescence of Cahokia must have involved a process of negotiations and agreements between different tribal groups or peoples, and that if the model of later peoples in this part of America is anything to go by, this process would have involved large public gatherings with massive feasts. Excavations of borrow pits near the plaza show the remains of such feasts. Pauketat's theory is that the Plaza was built to allow the holding of a great gathering/

feast/negotiation, which led to the creation of Cahokia. Once it was built, the plaza acted as a focal point for the Mississippian religion, providing a space for more feasts and gatherings and giving Cahokia a raison d'être. Once Cahokia was established, new hierarchies and social structures quickly became established, probably via the medium of gift-giving. Power in many tribal societies, especially in North America, often derives from the chief's ability to give things away, thus binding to him lower socio-economic groups, cementing allegiances and appeasing grievances and divisions.

The End of Cahokia

Many theories have been advanced to explain the decline and abandonment of Cahokia. Perhaps because they had no tradition of city-living, the Cahokians made little provision for mass sanitation, so the high population density must have led to disease. Overpopulation may also have stretched the ability of the surrounding area to feed the city (and there is evidence that satellite communities were set up specifically to cater for its needs). The high population and its consumption of wood may have led to deforestation, loss of biodiversity, soil erosion, flooding and rising water levels, all making it hard to sustain a city. Climate change, such as the cooling associated with the Little Ice Age from c 1250, may also have played a part. Increased warfare and conflict suggests that political changes were taking place, and perhaps challenges to Cahokia's authority. And if a settlement the size of Cahokia was unusual in Mississippian culture, perhaps it is not so surprising that once it declined, the population subsided back to a scattered, village-centred existence.

Cahokia declined in the 13th century, and it was essentially abandoned by the late 14th century. The Mississippian culture lived on in the southeastern USA, however, and it is thought likely that the Natchez Indians of Mississippi, described by Spanish and French explorers in the 16th to 18th centuries, may have been the

CHUNGKE

Plazas were probably used for feasts and ceremonies and may also have been used for playing chungke, a game still practised by Native Americans today. It involves a stone disc, which is rolled down the centre of a court, while the players throw javelin-like sticks, either to knock over the disc or to see who can land nearest to where it comes to a halt. In historical times players were known to wager all their worldly goods, down to the shirts off their backs, on the game of chungke. In Mound 72 at Cahokia, 15 chungke stones were found as part of a tribute cache to an early Cahokia leader.

inheritors of the Mississippian tradition. They lived in palisaded villages, played chungke, practised human sacrifice (the existence of which at Cahokia is attested to by headless and handless skeletons interred alongside nobles in burial mounds) and followed a solar religion.

Cahokia itself, however, attracted little attention and is still comparatively unknown. The mounds were treated with little respect by early settlers who flattened them to clear farmland, and even today much of Cahokia is built on and unprotected. There was also a trend among historians and archaeologists to deny or disparage the achievements of the Mississippians, with the mounds attributed to mythical pre-Columbian Europeans such as Phoenician or Welsh settlers, in keeping with the Manifest Destiny agenda that legitimized the dispossession of the indigenous peoples because of their 'primitive' nature.

Overleaf: Two of the lesser mounds in Cahokia Mounds State Historic Park. On the left is a platform mound, which may have had a structure on top of it, while on the right is a round-topped mound, used for burials.

PUEBLOS OF CHACO CANYON

LOCATION: NEW MEXICO, USA

DATE OF CONSTRUCTION: *c* 10TH CENTURY CE

ABANDONED: LATE 12TH CENTURY CE

BUILT BY: ANCESTRAL/ANCIENT PUEBLO PEOPLES (ALSO KNOWN AS ANASAZI)

KEY FEATURES: GREAT HOUSES; PUEBLO BONITO; KIVAS (CEREMONIAL CHAMBERS); TURQUOISE BEADS; ROAD SYSTEM

The US Army surveyors, cattle herders and cowboys of the 19th and 20th centuries who first sought to open up to settlement the arid canyons and deserts of (what is now) the Four Corners area of the Southwest USA were astonished to discover the remains of enormous buildings concealed within obscure canyons. Impressive multi-storey walls of stone and brick enclosed masses of rooms and chambers, in what are often described as apartment complexes. Who could have built such wonders and even more mysteriously, how could the large populations of these mini-metropolises possibly have been supported in the midst of a barren desert?

The desert canyons of the Southwest USA are deeply inhospitable. Today they support only a meagre population at an extremely low density, yet somehow this same area supported several complex societies centred on communities that may have numbered 10,000 or more. These communities vanished before Columbus, leaving the empty remnants of the largest buildings in pre-Columbian America – structures that would not be topped until the building of the first steel girder skyscrapers in Chicago in the 1880s. These buildings are known as Great Houses, and are the grandest form of pueblo, or village, constructed by the pre-Columbian inhabitants of the area. Although they are popularly known as the Anasazi, from the

Navajo word for 'ancient ones', the Navajo themselves were post-Columbian immigrants to the area, and archaeologists and historians now prefer to refer to the prehistoric residents as the Ancient Pueblo Peoples, or, in reference to their latter-day descendants the Hopi and Zuni (see below), the Ancestral Pueblo. The Anasazi were just one of several neighbouring cultures in this part of the Americas, but it is their remains that are the most noteworthy. Among these, the most impressive and best known are the cliff dwellings of Mesa Verde and the pueblos of Chaco Canyon (in northern New Mexico), which include the biggest Great House of all, known as Pueblo Bonito, and which constitute the largest cluster of archaeological remains in the USA.

Rise of the Ancestral Pueblo Peoples

Although the region was probably settled by hunter-gatherers from the time of the original peopling of the Americas (probably *c* 12000 BCE), it took a long time for agriculture to spread north from Mesoamerica. By the start of the Common Era crops such as corn, squash and beans were grown in the region by increasingly sedentary people and population densities began to increase. Around 600 CE farmers moved to Chaco Canyon, where they initially lived in underground pit houses, where a pit was dug, lined with flat stones,

walled with logs and roofed over with poles and woven matting. By around 700 CE they started to build stone structures above ground, eventually adopting an accomplished form of rubble-core dry-stone masonry, where carefully selected and shaped brick-like stones are used to form twin veneers, the space between which is filled with rubble and adobe. By 920 CE buildings at Pueblo Bonito were two storeys high, and from around 1000 CE Chaco Canyon Anasazi culture reached its climax, although it lasted for only a brief period until its catastrophic collapse in around 1150 CE.

At its height Chaco Canyon was a thriving population hub centred on Pueblo Bonito and 12 other Great Houses along the canyon, spaced at intervals of about a

Pueblo Bonito Great House in Chaco Canyon. The large round structures are kivas. Note the wall running towards the camera across the central plaza, with a kiva on either side. This wall runs north-south and divides the pueblo in two.

mile. Holes in the canyon's northern walls, drilled for wooden roof beams, show that much of its length was lined with houses, while the remains of hundreds of small settlements have been found on the canyon's southern side. Taken together with the size of Great Houses like Pueblo Bonito (see below), this would seem to indicate that up to 10,000 or more people lived here. On the other hand, the consensus among most archaeologists is that even with the Anasazi's expertise at

Across the canyon from Pueblo Bonito is a giant subterranean kiva called Casa Rinconada, precisely arranged along a north-south axis. Around the walls are 28 niches and six crypts. At the summer solstice a beam of sunlight coming through the northeastern entrance illuminates one of the niches. It seems likely that this is an accident, though, and that when the kiva was in use this alignment would have been impossible to see because structural beams and other rooms probably blocked the light.

dryland agriculture, the meagre natural resources of the region would have limited the maximum population to less than 5,000 and this would appear to be borne out by the finding that many of the rooms in Pueblo Bonito were unoccupied for long stretches of time. One suggestion is that the Great Houses were ceremonial centres that were only periodically occupied and that the permanent population of the canyon was relatively low, swelling on special occasions.

Chaco Canyon was also the hub of a sophisticated network of roads that linked it to tens of thousands of smaller Anasazi settlements across the Four Corners region; 22,000 have been identified in New Mexico alone. The roads are up to 96 kilometres (59½ miles) long and 13 metres (42½ feet) wide and some still show evidence of stone kerbs, indicating that they were carefully constructed and maintained. The presence of trade goods at Pueblo Bonito shows that these roads were used to import food, timber and other raw materials, particularly luxury goods such as turquoise, shells and even exotic bird feathers from as far away as Mexico. The roads may also have had military uses, allowing the rapid transit of soldiers directed from the centre of power at Chaco Canyon.

An alternative point of view, however, is that the roads were primarily religious or spiritual in significance and function. Unlike most Native American roads, they do not follow the contours of the landscape or detour around obstructions; rather they run in straight lines, converging on Chaco Canyon like spokes on a wheel. One theory is that the roads were sacred highways and functioned as ceremonial routes and religious symbols. The writer Paul Devereux has shown that many different cultures in history have shared the concept of ghost or spirit roads – actual geographical routes that spirits follow, including the souls of the dead, shamans on spirit quests and other supernatural entities – and that the defining characteristic of these is that they run in straight lines. Given the suspected importance of Chaco Canyon as a spiritual and religious centre for the Anasazi, is it possible that they built these roads to facilitate the free passage of spirits to and from their natural home (thus helping to propitiate and draw power from them)?

Pueblo Bonito

The jewel in the Anasazi crown was the Great House at Pueblo Bonito. This was the biggest Anasazi structure. It was up to six storeys high and comprised over 600 rooms, all jumbled together into a contiguous structure not dissimilar to Çatalhöyük (see page 16), with entrance to upper levels via flat roofs, which themselves were the site of communal activities. It was built with timber roof supports made from huge single logs up to 5 metres (16 feet) long, weighing as much as 317.5 kilograms (700 pounds). Over 200,000 of them were used in the construction of the Chaco Canyon pueblos, which took shape over the course of two centuries. At first, pinyon pines from the local area were used, but when these were exhausted the Anasazi had to look further afield. Analysis of mineral isotopes in surviving timbers has allowed experts to determine the exact locations these logs came from – the Chuska and San Mateo mountains, around

80.5 kilometres (50 miles) away. The Anasazi had no carts or pack animals, so they would have had to bring the logs down from the mountains by muscle power alone. The timber, well preserved in the dry desert air, has also helped archaeologists to date the settlements through the science of dendrochronology – counting tree rings to determine dates and also information about climate.

Most of the rooms in Pueblo Bonito are around 4 x 5 metres (13 x 16 feet), but there are several large circular chambers called 'kivas' after contemporary Native American structures that seem to be identical. Contemporary kivas are used for rituals and tribal gatherings and it is assumed that Anasazi kivas served similar functions. Other rooms in the pueblo were food storage chambers, while beneath the floors of some rooms were burials complete with rich grave goods, including great quantities of valuable turquoise beads. The skeletons of those buried here are taller and larger than at lesser Anasazi sites, suggesting that the well-fed Anasazi elite lived in the Great Houses and were supported by the produce and labour of the lower orders who dwelt at outlying settlements.

Seeds of Destruction

Two of the greatest mysteries regarding Chaco Canyon and the Anasazi are how they supported a dense population in such a barren region and why their civilization collapsed. The two are probably closely linked. The upland desert of the Four Corners region appears to be highly unsuitable for agriculture. Rainfall is low, sporadic and unpredictable, and tends to occur in sudden intense bursts that cause flash flooding where most of the runoff is lost. Temperatures at high elevations, where rainfall is higher, are very low and the conditions mean that forest growth and soil fertility replenishment are slow.

The Anasazi used several techniques to overcome the limits of the environment. They devised sophisticated water management schemes in Chaco Canyon, damming

the main canyon and feeder canyons to catch and store runoff. They grew crops at sites such as the alluvial bottom of Chaco Canyon where the water table was close enough to the surface for the roots of their crops to reach and they founded agricultural colonies or stations over a wide area so that at least some of them would garner enough rainfall to produce a surplus big enough for redistribution.

But in the success of the Chaco Canyon Anasazi lay the seeds of their downfall. Their system of agriculture was marginal – in good years, with decent rainfall, it could support a large population, but they could only store corn for two years (after this it will rot and become inedible), making them vulnerable to drought. At the same time, the urban model they adopted at Chaco Canyon was unsustainable in this impoverished ecosystem. Analysis of plant remains in packrat middens (nests of dried litter left by packrats, which can survive for thousands of years in the desert) has shown that after 1000 CE the Chaco Canyon Anasazi had deforested the local area, which in turn led to problems with soil erosion and loss of fertility. Eventually Chaco Canyon became a largely unproductive centre, dependent on the rest of the wider Anasazi world to supply it with everything from food and timber to luxury goods, presumably because by then the Anasazi had developed a strict hierarchical society centred on the canyon and the elite who lived in the Great Houses.

By the 12th century the growing environmental problems caused by the dense population combined with a prolonged drought period caused the collapse of the Chaco Canyon Anasazi. Dendrochronology shows that the last timber used at Pueblo Bonito was cut in 1117, while the youngest anywhere in the Canyon dates to 1170. Other Anasazi sites show evidence of fortification, warfare and cannibalism, and it seems likely that as crops failed and famine spread, the centre could not hold and the society descended into disorder and warfare. Some of the Anasazi appear to have survived by moving to new areas and the lack of useful artefacts at many Anasazi sites

Above: Explorer ascending to an Ancestral Pueblo cliff dwelling, built, like the far larger Cliff Palace, into an alcove in the cliff. In the 19th and early 20th century, many Ancestral Pueblo sites were visited and stripped by looters. Opposite: Part of Cliff Palace at Mesa Verde, the largest cliff dwelling in North America. Like Chaco Canyon, Mesa Verde was an important population centre for the Ancestral Pueblo.

shows that the residents effected a planned evacuation, taking their important objects with them. It is believed that the Pueblo Peoples, including the Hopi, Zuni and Acoma, who still live in pueblos and practice dryland agriculture, are at least partly descended from the Anasazi.

TENOCHTITLÁN

LOCATION: VALLEY OF MEXICO, MEXICO
DATE OF CONSTRUCTION: 1325 CE
ABANDONED: 1521
BUILT BY: AZTECS
KEY FEATURES: MAIN TEMPLE PYRAMIDS; CANALS AND CAUSEWAYS; GREAT MARKET; AQUEDUCTS; PUBLIC LATRINES; CHINAMPAS 'FLOATING FIELDS'

When Hernán Cortés and his small band of conquistadors first saw the Aztec capital of Tenochtitlán, they were astonished. Its sheer size astounded them, for it was four times as big as the largest city in Spain (Seville), bigger even than Paris or Venice, the greatest cities in Europe. In appearance it surpassed even these urban marvels. Appearing to float on a huge lake, the city was of pristine white, interlaced with a grid of canals, causeways and streets, all of which led to a huge precinct in the centre of town where broad plazas surrounded towering pyramids of vivid red and blue, encrusted with ornate sculptures. All was clean, spacious and orderly.

Bernal Diaz del Castillo, one of Cortés's soldiers who later penned an account of the conquest of Mexico, wrote that it, 'seemed like an enchanted vision… Indeed some of our soldiers asked whether it was not all a dream… It was all so wonderful that I do not know how to describe this first glimpse of things never heard of, seen, or dreamed of before.' But just two years later all this would be gone, razed to the ground after a desperate and bitter siege. 'Of all the wonders I beheld that day, nothing now remains. All is overthrown and lost,' lamented Diaz, who had himself taken part in the methodical, house-by-house destruction of the greatest city in pre-Columbian America.

City of the Mexica

Tenochtitlán is known today as the capital of the Aztec Empire, but the term 'Aztec' is problematic. In Náhuatl, the language of the Aztecs, it means 'people of Aztlán', referring to the legendary homeland from which several tribes emigrated to the lands in and around the Valley of Mexico. The founders of Tenochtitlán called themselves the Mexica, and according to their foundation myth, they had followed their sun/war god (possibly a mythologized war chief) Huitzilopochtli to the shores of Lake Texcoco, where he tossed the heart of a conquered enemy into the waters and commanded them to make their home at the spot where it landed. There the Mexica found an eagle, wrestling with a snake and perched on a cactus growing out of a rock – a vision commemorated as the national emblem of Mexico – and accordingly named their new home the 'Place of the Fruit of the Cactus': Tenochtitlán.

Whatever their origins, the Mexica were one of a number of tribes who moved into the Valley of Mexico region to fill the vacuum left by the collapse of the Toltecs in the 11th century CE. Arriving relatively late

A woodcut of a map of Tenochtitlán, based on an illustration from a letter sent by Hernán Cortés to the King of Spain relating his achievements and the story of his conquests. The illustration is said to have been drawn up by Cortés himself.

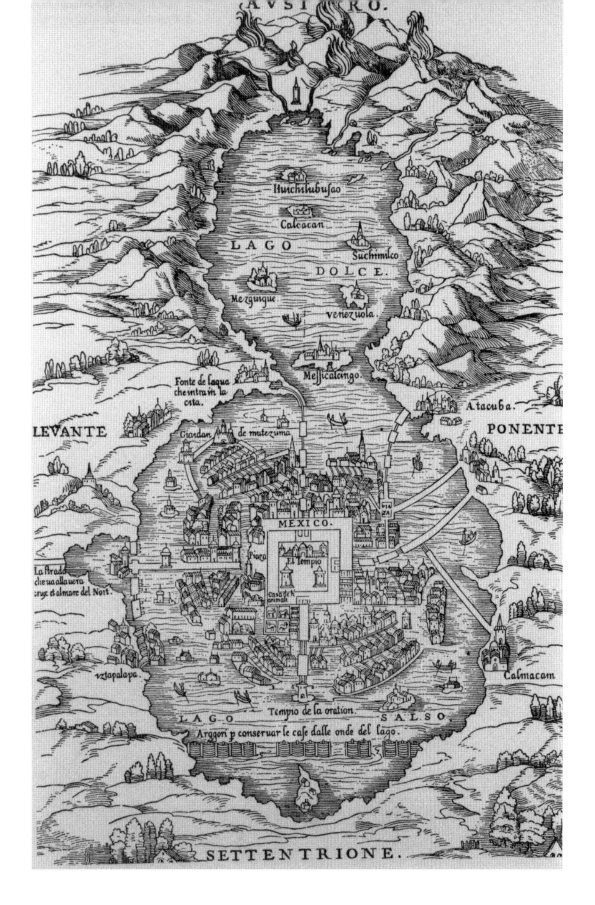

(1325) they were stuck with one of the apparently less desirable sites – a marshy island in the middle of the partly brackish lake. Through a combination of warrior spirit, agricultural technology and religious zeal, they overcame their humble origins.

The original island was drained and extended through land reclamation and clever swampland agriculture, and joined to the neighbouring island city-state of Tlatelolco. Mexica nobles bolstered their power through marriage into old Toltec noble lineages and political alliances, and in the 15th century established a triple alliance with two other Aztec city-states, going on to conquer the Valley of Mexico and territories beyond. As the empire grew, Tenochtitlán came to dominate, the city and its emperor – the 'great speaker' or *huei tlatoque* – sitting atop a socio-economic pyramid of political power and tribute. Conquered kings and princes were allowed to retain control of their city-states, in return for the payment of tribute. They in turn were supported by the tribute of lesser nobles and so on down to the common class, who generated this tribute through their agricultural and industrial labour, mainly the production of cotton textiles through cottage industry (in fact, all Aztec women, from slaves to princesses, spun and wove cotton). Four times a year vast quantities of tribute streamed into Tenochtitlán.

Tenochtitlán at Its Peak

At first the island city grew organically and haphazardly, but after a major flood the Mexica took the opportunity to rebuild along carefully planned lines, perhaps inspired by the ruins of ancient Teotihuacán to the northeast. The new city was laid out on a grid of orthogonal streets and canals, with four main processional ways dividing it into quarters, which themselves were divided into smaller neighbourhoods called *calpulli*. Each *calpulli* had its own local temples and markets, and each was organized around a tightly knit hierarchy of family and clan networks. The fifth district of the city, reflecting the fifth cardinal direction that the Mesoamericans recognized, was the centre, where heaven and Earth came together at a sort of *axis mundi* (offering clear parallels with ancient Babylon – see page 28).

Here the Mexica constructed a great sacred precinct, surrounded by a wall of carved serpents, 347.5 x 301.75 metres (380 x 330 yards) in area and with room for more than 8,000 people. Within stood huge stone pyramids, including the Main Temple. About 27 metres (more than 90 feet) high, the Main Temple consisted of two stepped pyramids side by side on a huge platform. They symbolized the two sacred mountains of Aztec myth; the homes of the two central deities of their pantheon. The southern pyramid was sacred to Huitzilopochtli ('Hummingbird Left') and represented Coatepec, or Snake Mountain, where he had sprung fully armed from his mother's womb and destroyed his evil sister. The northern pyramid symbolized Tonacatepetl, the Edenic fertile mountain paradise home of Tlaloc ('Long Cave'), the god of fertility that the Aztecs had appropriated from the Toltecs. Thus, like the Khmer at Angkor Wat (see page 136), the Mexica had transformed the heart of their capital into a sacred landscape that celebrated and affirmed their claim to dominion, specifically their military power, through the war god Huitzilopochtli, and their economic power, through the god Tlaloc, who brought natural plenty.

The rise to power of the Aztecš was accompanied by a remarkable population explosion in and around the Valley of Mexico. In the early Aztec period (1150–1350 CE) the Valley had a population of *c* 175,000. By the late Aztec period (1350–1519 CE) it had increased to nearly a million, with around 200,000 people living in Tenochtitlán alone, making it one of the largest cities in the world at the time. According to the Spanish, who were welcomed, albeit warily, to the city and initially viewed it as awestruck tourists, the great market in the city attracted crowds of up to 60,000 people – more people than lived in the biggest city in Spain. Here they observed women taking an equal part in many aspects of life, including trading; gaudily made-up prostitutes loudly chewing a form of gum to attract customers; humble commoners; haughty warriors and priests and an astonishing profusion of food and other goods from across America, including seafood from both the Pacific and Atlantic coasts, exotic animals and birds from the jungles to the south, obsidian blades from the north and possibly even goods from the Inca Empire to the far south.

The Spaniards were also struck by the cleanliness of the city. Aqueducts brought fresh water to the city and the residents bathed at least once a day. There were no pack animals to foul the streets and each house was equipped with private latrines, while public toilets, in the form of latrines over barges, covered over for privacy, were moored at intervals along canals throughout the city. Human waste collected in this orderly fashion was transported by canal to the fields on the edges of the city. These fields, called *chinampas*, are often described as floating gardens, and it was even said they could be untethered and moved. This is probably an exaggeration. In practice, the *chinampas* were an ingenious way of converting the limitations of the swamp setting into a highly productive form of intensive agriculture. A rectangular patch of swamp was enclosed by wattle fences between stakes and then the level within raised with dredged mud, decaying vegetation and human ordure as fertilizer. Long rows of these small fields were separated by a grid of canals that controlled irrigation, forming productive market gardens and reclaiming the swamp.

Downfall

In less than two centuries Tenochtitlán had grown from an obscure swamp town to arguably the greatest city on Earth, in what Inga Clendinnen of LaTrobe University in Australia describes as, 'a remarkable experiment in urban living', based on quite different principles to those that governed European cities. Rather than being depersonalizing, individualizing and democratizing, it was close knit with rigid hierarchies, strong family and clan ties. Rather then being porous and chaotic it was strictly monitored and controlled, with heavy restrictions on free movement. Rather than being dirty and ramshackle it was clean and ordered. And rather than tending to promote secularity it revolved around religion, including a constant stream of gory bloodletting and human sacrifice. The Aztecs believed themselves to be the chosen people, with a destiny to rule and to take responsibility for the proper functioning of both heaven and Earth, including the passage of the sun across the sky, and this required blood.

To the Spanish all this was alien and wrong, and their hostility was inflamed by their lust for gold. They moved into the palace as 'honoured guests', but in reality they made the Aztec emperor, Moctezuma, their virtual prisoner, and issued increasingly strident demands for lavish gifts of gold. The conquistador leader Cortés and his priests started to throw their weight around with regards to the replacement of Aztec idols with Christian symbols. Tenochtitlán rapidly became a powder-keg, which was ignited when Cortés' lieutenant, Pedro de Alvarado, had hundreds of Aztec nobles massacred. The Indians rose up in revolt, laying siege to the embattled Spaniards. Moctezuma was sent out to calm the people, but was met with a hail of stones. The Spaniards claim he died from these injuries, but it is more likely that he was murdered now that he was of no more use. On July 1st, 1520, the Spaniards made a desperate night flit, only to return a year later with an army of Spanish soldiers and native allies, and lay siege to the city. Convinced of their divine mission, the Aztecs hung on, but with their ranks decimated by smallpox brought by the invaders, defeat was inevitable. Cortés levelled the city and built a new one on top. Today the site of Tenochtitlán lies at the heart of Mexico City and the Valley of Mexico once again hosts one of the largest cities on Earth.

CHICHEN ITZA

LOCATION: YUCATÁN PENINSULA, MEXICO

DATE OF CONSTRUCTION: *c* 600 CE

ABANDONED: 1000 OR 1250 CE

BUILT BY: MAYA

KEY FEATURES: SACRED CENOTE; EL CASTILLO PYRAMID; EL CARACOL OBSERVATORY; HIGH PRIEST'S TEMPLE; CASA DEL MONJAS; GREAT BALL COURT; CHAC MOOL STATUES

The greatest city of the northern Maya, located in Mexico's Yucatán peninsula, Chichen Itza is today one of the most famous and most visited of their ancient relics, celebrated for its pyramids, its Great Ball Court and for the brooding cenote, or water-filled sinkhole, which gives the city its name and made it a site of religious importance and pilgrimage long after its collapse.

Chichen Itza means 'at the mouth of the well of Itza', the 'well' being the Cenote Sagrado, or Sacred Cenote, also known as the Cenote of Sacrifice, into which, according to Mayan legends recorded in post-Columbian times, human sacrifices were flung to intercede with the subterranean gods. In Spanish the city's name is often written as Chichén Itzá, the accents showing that the stress should be placed on the second syllables of each word. This is standard pronunciation practice for Yucatec Mayan, the language of the local people today, and probably the language spoken by their ancestors who built the city. To be even more correct, the name should be written as Chich'en Itza, the apostrophe signifying a glottal sound in the pronunciation of *ch'en* ('well').

Maya of the North

The Maya were the most sophisticated pre-Columbian culture in the Americas, the only one with a fully-developed system of writing, along with all the other characteristics shared by Mesoamerican civilizations, such as monumental architecture, advanced astronomy and mathematics and highly developed water management. It spread its influence across a wide zone from the southern states of Mexico to Guatemala and Belize. What is known as the Classic period of Mayan civilization began in around 250 CE, centred on the southern zone of the Mayan heartland, with city-states such as Palenque, Copán and Tikal (see page 170). These collapsed dramatically in the 9th century, after which the northern lowlands of the Yucatán, and Chichen Itza in particular, took over the mantle of the leading Mayan city-states.

Chichen Itza itself became a significant city sometime around 600 CE and the architectural styles it displays suggest a mixed heritage of Mayan and other influences, including 'Mexican' ones (i.e. from the Valley of Mexico, where pre-Aztec civilizations such as the Toltecs were coeval with the Maya). According to the *Chilam Balam*, a history written by Mayan sources after the Spanish conquest had begun, the city took its name from a group of 'foreigners' known as the Itza, who spoke only a broken version of Maya. It is thought that this might be a reference to a group known as the Chontal Maya from areas to the west, in the modern Mexican states of Tabasco and Campeche, who spoke a

different dialect of Maya. They would have had contact with Mexican cultures and hence could have introduced these influences to Chichen Itza.

The *Chilam Balam* goes on to relate how, in the 10th century CE, a group of 'Toltec' immigrants from the west led by Kukulcan (the Maya name for the god known to the Aztecs as Quetzlcoatl), took over the city and remade it in an even more 'Mexicanized' style, as a Toltec city. But the archaeological record seems to tell a slightly different tale, because there is evidence of a major population influx in the 9th rather than 10th century, corresponding with the collapse of the Classic sites in the southern lowlands (see page 173) – presumably people fleeing famine and warfare made their way north to city-states less affected by the drought that is

The Sacred Cenote that gives Chichen Itza its name. Valuables and human sacrifices were tossed in to appease and intercede with the gods of the underworld.

thought to have triggered the Classic collapse (see below for the reason for this).

There is also uncertainty about what happened to Chichen Itza to cause its decline and eventual abandonment. The traditional account is that the city rose to prominence in the 9th century and became the leading power of what is known as the Late/Terminal Classic period. This does not necessarily mean that it was the capital of a Mayan empire, because the lack of pack animals and the limitations of Mayan agriculture tended to restrict the military reach of Mayan city-states, so that the control of any one king could not extend much further than his own power base. But Chichen Itza was the dominant force in the region, its authority possibly bolstered by the prestige of its Sacred Cenote. After two centuries of this hegemony, it lost control after a civil war, recorded in the Mayan chronicles, which eventually led to the razing of the city in around 1250 CE, testified to by the burnt remnants of some of the temples atop its pyramids.

More recently, however, this chronology has been challenged, with dating of the site by radiocarbon dating and analysis of ceramic styles suggesting that it actually collapsed in around 1000 CE, just when it was previously thought to have been at the height of its power. Such an early date would also seem to rule out Toltec influence on the city, since the Toltecs did not flourish until after this date. Whatever the actual date of its decline, Mayan sources suggest that the site was not forgotten because of the Sacred Cenote, which pilgrims continued to visit.

The Sacred Cenote

The key to Chichen Itza's power was its cenotes. The northern lowlands of Yucatán can be arid, with rainfall coming intermittently and unpredictably (and often destructively, in the form of hurricanes), and no rivers or streams of any sort. The strange geology of the region, with porous and easily eroded karst limestone, which is low-lying and thus very close to the water table, means, however, that water is accessible through the cenotes and these supplied the Maya with water and made it possible to support sizeable populations in an otherwise inhospitable region.

The head of a feathered serpent looks out over the Great Ball Court, the largest Mesoamerican ball court, where teams competed to knock a heavy rubber ball around the court. The losers could suffer a grisly forfeit – murals show the victorious captain decapitating his foe.

The Sacred Cenote is a particularly large example. It is almost perfectly circular, with a diameter of more than 50 metres (164 feet) and a 20-metre (65½-feet) drop to the murky green water, which itself is at least 15 metres (49 feet) deep, with a bottom of thick slime and mud. Chroniclers of the post-Columbian era recorded that the Maya would make offerings and sacrifices to the rain god Chaac, hoping that they would intercede with him and gain his favour. In particular, they would throw in young maidens. Sometimes several would be tossed in at dawn and any who survived until midday would be hauled out and interrogated about what they had seen, relating lurid stories of their exchanges with those who dwelt in the black depths of the well.

Inspired by these tales, in 1894 Edward Thompson, the American consul in the nearby town of Merida, purchased the land on which Chichen Itza's ruins stood and determined to make a remarkable investigation of the depths of the Sacred Cenote. He brought in dredging equipment and spent years scooping foul muck from its bottom, having calculated the correct spot to explore by throwing corpse-sized logs from the rim to see where they landed and sank. He successfully brought up a range of artefacts, including spears, axe heads, copper discs, pottery and votive offerings such as jade ornaments and small gold bells. The ornaments had been deliberately broken and the bells flattened, perhaps as a way of symbolically 'killing' them. He also brought up large numbers of balls of copal incense, which was burned during sacrifices, and the bones of many young women and other victims.

Finally, when it appeared that the scoop was striking bedrock, he donned a heavy diving suit and had himself lowered into the inky black depths. Groping around he discovered that he was at the bottom of a huge, deep well scooped out of the thick mud. 'I felt a strange thrill when I realized that I was the only living being who had ever reached this place alive and expected to leave it

again still living,' he reported in his 1933 book *People of the Serpent*. By probing with his fingers in the crevices of the rocky bottom he was able to bring up many small artefacts of copper, gold and jade.

Buildings of Chichen Itza
Chichen Itza has an 'old town', known as Old Chichen, where temples and structures are located, but the most impressive ruins (many of them restored) are in the newer city. It is dominated by the great stepped pyramid of Kukulcan, known as El Castillo ('the castle'). A stairway runs up each of the four sides, climbing up nine platforms to a height of 25 metres (82 feet). The pyramid is aligned so that at the spring equinox the corner of the pyramid casts a snakelike shadow onto its northern face, which 'slithers' as the sun progresses across the sky (attracting huge crowds of tourists). Buried within is another, older pyramid, with a chamber within containing a jaguar-shaped throne and a Chac Mool statue. Chac Mool statues are reclining figures with dishes for offerings in their laps, first discovered at this site.

A smaller but similar pyramid is known as the High Priest's Temple, because when Thompson investigated it he found what he took to be the burial chamber of a priest. In fact he found a descending series of burial chambers, starting at the top of the pyramid. Sounding the floor with a steel rod he detected a void beneath and pried up the flagstone, accessing another chamber. He repeated this through five tombs until he penetrated a space carved into the rock below the pyramid, which was full of ash and heat-fused jade beads. In an evocative passage he describes what happened when he lifted a slab in the corner of this chamber, expecting to find only a heap of ashes beneath: 'It yielded so suddenly that I fell back with it… My companions also fell back, for it disclosed a big, circular, pitch-black hole… [from which] came a… cold, damp wind… The two natives [his companions] were simply glued to their places in sheer terror. Finally Pedro spoke. "It is the mouth of Hell."' In fact it was a 15.25-metre (50-foot) deep pit, and in true Indiana Jones style, Thompson had himself lowered into it to discover that it was crawling with toxic spiders guarding a collection of mortuary artefacts.

Other important buildings are the Temple of the Warriors, a stepped pyramid with rows of carved columns showing warriors, similar to Toltec structures at the city of Tula. A building known as La Casa del Monjas ('the nunnery') because it was thought to have been a sort of convent for an order of priestesses and female initiates, it is now understood to have been a governmental building. To the north of this is El Caracol ('the snail'), a round building on a square platform named for the spiral stone staircase that winds up the interior of the building. It resembles a modern-day observatory and indeed was used for this purpose by the Maya.

To the northwest of the castle is the Great Ball Court, the largest such court ever discovered. It is 175 metres (574 feet) long and 70 metres (229½ feet) wide, making it bigger than an American football field, and has 7-metre (23-feet) high walls along each side, decorated with carvings of teams of players, including a grisly depiction of what happened to the losers of the Mesoamerican ball game. This was played with a heavy ball of rubber, which players kept aloft with their forearms, hips and thighs, possibly with the aim of scoring

One of the hoops or rings set into the walls of the Great Ball Court. Although this is called a 'scoring ring', it is not actually known how the Maya ball game was played or what the precise role of the ring was, no matter how appealing the apparent parallel with basketball. The ring is set high in the side-wall, and knocking the heavy rubber ball through it would have been a feat of tremendous skill.

through hoops, two of which are set into the tops of the court's side-walls. In one of the carvings the captain of the defeated team is shown decapitated, with jets of blood spurting from his neck.

TIKAL

LOCATION: GUATEMALA

DATE OF CONSTRUCTION: *c* 200 BCE

ABANDONED: *c* 900 CE

BUILT BY: MAYA

KEY FEATURES: GREAT PLAZA; MANY STEPPED PYRAMIDS; BALL COURTS; PALACES; STELAE

The largest and greatest Maya city, Tikal was so utterly abandoned that it was not fully rediscovered until 1848. Yet more than 60,000 people – perhaps up to 200,000 – lived in a city that covered over 121.75 square kilometres (47 square miles), and which dominated the Mayan heartland from the Yucatán to western Honduras. Only recently has decipherment of the mysterious Mayan script made it possible to read the wealth of inscriptions (known as 'glyphs') at the site, revealing the city's bloody history of violence and intrigue.

Tikal in Guatemala was the greatest city of the greatest era of Maya history, the Classic period. The name by which it is known today is a relatively recent appellation, meaning 'at the waterhole', a reference to the semi-artificial reservoirs the ancient Maya constructed to help control the water supply that made their intensive agriculture and very high population densities possible. According to the glyphs at the site, the city's inhabitants called it Yax Mutul, and the glyph for *mutul*, thought to represent a top-knot of hair, itself probably symbolic of a sacred corn sheaf, has been found on stones in cities throughout the region, testament to the city's long reach.

The Rise and Fall and Rise of Tikal

The first settlement of Tikal dates back to 800 BCE, but the city only properly began to take shape around 200 BCE,

with the laying down of Tikal's urban core, particularly what would become the Great Plaza. This was a large flat area covered in plaster, which remained the city's hub for a thousand years. Tikal's glory days coincided with the Classic period of Maya civilization, from around 250–900 CE. Although Maya writing long predates this, the first dated inscription at Tikal – indeed the first one found in the Maya heartland – dates to 292 CE (or 8.12.14.13.15 in the Maya Long Count calendar). It is written on a *stela*, an inscribed upright slab of stone, of which dozens were erected at Tikal, with about 70 in the Great Plaza alone. By reading these *stelae*, and inscriptions on temple doorway lintels and other sources, historians have been able to piece together a very precisely dated list of kings and queens, in the process uncovering a tale of dynastic politics and inter-city rivalry that saw Tikal become the pre-eminent Maya city. By controlling the lucrative trans-isthmus trade routes and through force of arms, Tikal dominated most of the Maya heartland.

The inscriptions show that one of Tikal's most revered rulers, Jaguar Paw (this was the initial interpretation of his

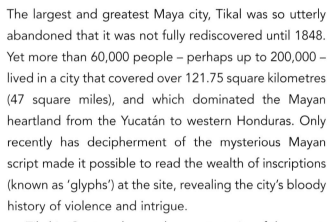

The North Acropolis, the ritual centre of Tikal – one of several groups of pyramids and other monumental structures, raised above the swampy forest floor and linked by plazas and causeways, which make up the Maya city.

Temple One on the Great Plaza, one of the greatest achievements of the Maya Tikal, built after the city's return to dominance in the Late Classic Period. Facing west towards the setting sun, Temple One was considered to be a portal to the underworld.

was an increase in conflict with its neighbours, which eventually led to the establishment of an alliance between Tikal's enemies. Glyphs from Tikal and other sites enable us to trace the politics of this era in fine detail. It seems that its traditional enemy, the city-state of Calakmul, was able to capitalize on a fatal misjudgement by the rulers of Tikal, who sprang a surprise raid on their erstwhile ally Caracol in 556 CE. Nursing resentment, Caracol allied with Calakmul, and waited until a favourable astronomical alignment to begin its revenge. Caracol's sorcerer-priest-astronomers declared that the most auspicious moment was when Venus rose in its closest conjunction with the dawn sun, which came to pass in 562. With Calakmul's help, Caracol launched a devastating raid on Tikal and in the decades that followed the Calakmul-Caracol axis cemented the suppression of Tikal by engineering alliances with other city-states previously under Tikal's control. Finally, in the late 6th century, Calakmul supported a breakaway clique of Tikal nobles who set up a rival city at Dos Pilas, which called itself New Tikal.

By the late 6th century Tikal was entirely ringed by hostile city-states, and for over a century no inscriptions were made at Tikal, a period of 'silence' known as the Tikal Hiatus. It marks the transition from the Early to Late Classic period and when Tikal finally re-established itself, the nature of Maya culture had changed, with Teotihuacán elements expunged.

In 672 Tikal began its resurgence with a campaign against Dos Pilas and over the next 100 years Tikal regained much of its former power and reached the height of its magnificence. More and more grand buildings were erected on raised platforms or acropolises around the city centre – more than 3,000 in total – including monstrous stepped pyramids up to 64 metres (210 feet) high. There are also numerous palaces (which may in fact be government/administrative buildings), ball courts, causeways, observatories and domestic buildings.

name based on the appearance of his glyphs; now that they can be read properly it is known that his name was Chak Tok Ich'aak I) died on 31 January, 378 CE, on the same day that Siyah K'ak', a lord from the 'Mexican' city of Teotihuacán (see page 162), arrived. It is hard to avoid the conclusion that 31 January 378 was the exact date of a battle in which Siyah K'ak', a conquering general from Teotihuacán, defeated and slew Jaguar Paw.

Tikal now fell under Teotihuacán influence, with Mexicanized architecture and the introduction of a military innovation, the spear-thrower. The long-term result

By 750 CE Tikal was at its peak, but little more than a century later the city faced a catastrophic collapse. The last dated *stela* erected at Tikal is dated 869, while the last to be found anywhere in the southern lowlands dates to 909. What could have happened to lay low a civilization at the height of its powers, in what University of Pennsylvania archaeologist Robert Sharer calls 'one of the most profound cultural failures in human history'?

Heading for a Fall

Tikal's achievements were possible because of its burgeoning population, which seemed to defy the environment as it appears today. Despite the lush forest that surrounds the city, the southern lowlands where Tikal is sited do not provide the most promising environment for the agricultural base needed to support an advanced civilization. Rainfall is highly variable, with long dry seasons, there are few rivers and, except in valley bottoms, the soils are thin and slow to replenish fertility. Until relatively recently the area was very sparsely populated. Tikal itself was so utterly abandoned that in 1525 when Hernán Cortés marched through the region, he passed unaware within a few miles of the city. In 1841, during their survey of dozens of Mayan sites, pioneering explorers John Lloyd Stephens and Frederick Catherwood missed it entirely. So how was it possible for a city of over 60,000 people to have existed here a thousand years earlier?

At Tikal the Maya sought to overcome these limitations by adapting natural depressions and excavating new ones to create massive reservoirs – big enough to hold enough drinking water to meet the needs of 10,000 people for up to 18 months. They also adopted agricultural innovations, such as mulching to preserve moisture and fertilize fields, multiple cropping in a single year and timing the planting of crops to make maximum use of heavy rains and floods. Intensive agriculture produced high yields and they were able to support steadily increasing population densities of up to 1,500 people per square mile (for comparison, this is twice that of the most densely populated countries in Africa today and orders of magnitude above what the same landscape supported well into the 20th century).

But this drive to maximize the intensity and productivity of their agriculture put the Maya on a collision course with nature. Although the relatively scarce valley bottoms of the southern lowlands could maintain a reasonable level of fertility and, crucially, a reasonable rate of replenishment of that fertility, the marginal zones that the Maya increasingly looked to exploit could not. With population growth came additional pressures on the environment. Forest clearance for agriculture was exacerbated by wood cutting for construction, firewood and the production of plaster, with which the Maya were obsessed (they used it as a means of beautifying their edifices). Deforestation led to soil erosion, flash floods, loss of water retention and eventually to climate change through reduced rainfall. Replenishment of soil fertility collapsed and the population was forced to rely on the overextended core arable land of the valley bottoms.

Proxy climate records, such as sediments deposited in lake beds, reveal that this period also saw one of the most severe and extended dry periods for over a thousand years, with particular peaks in drought conditions around 810, 860 and 910. Environmental breakdown had probably already led to tension over diminishing land and food resources, and the severe droughts plunged the Classic Maya into a catastrophic collapse. Authority broke down, conflict raged and millions starved. The archaeological evidence shows that palaces and government buildings at Tikal were burned and it is not hard to imagine a vengeful populace turning on the rulers whose covenant with their people was to ensure prosperity in return for obeisance. By the end of the 10th century, what was the greatest American metropolis of its age had been completely abandoned, after a collapse that many see as a grim warning to our modern unsustainable society.

TIWANAKU

LOCATION: LAKE TITICACA, BOLIVIA

DATE OF CONSTRUCTION: *c* 200 CE

ABANDONED: *c* 1000 CE

BUILT BY: TIWANAKU CIVILIZATION (AYMARA?)

KEY FEATURES: GATEWAY OF THE SUN; AKAPANA PYRAMID;
SEMI-SUBTERRANEAN TEMPLE; KALASASAYA TEMPLE; SOPHISTICATED
DRY-STONE MASONRY; MONOLITHS AND STELAE; SUKA KOLLUS
RAISED FIELDS

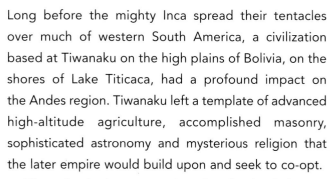

Long before the mighty Inca spread their tentacles over much of western South America, a civilization based at Tiwanaku on the high plains of Bolivia, on the shores of Lake Titicaca, had a profound impact on the Andes region. Tiwanaku left a template of advanced high-altitude agriculture, accomplished masonry, sophisticated astronomy and mysterious religion that the later empire would build upon and seek to co-opt.

Tiwanaku is the name given by the local Aymara people to the monumental ruins about 15 kilometres (9¼ miles) from the southeastern shore of Lake Titicaca, about 72 kilometres (44¾ miles) west of La Paz in Bolivia. In Spanish, the ruined city and the modern town that has developed at the site are known as Tiahuanaco. What its builders called it is not known. From around 200 CE to around 1000, Tiwanaku was the centre of a major civilization, possibly an empire (see below), which spread its influence across a broad swathe of the Andean region, as far as southern Peru, northern Chile and even Argentina. They left impressive monuments of stone and earth, including pyramids, temples, colossal statues and *stelae*. At 3,850 metres (12,631 feet) above sea level, it may have been the highest capital city in history. In recent decades it has become a major national and international tourist attraction, its monuments symbols of Bolivian national identity, but the site faces increasingly challenging issues.

Challenges of the Altiplano

The high plateau between the western and eastern ranges of the Andes is known as the Altiplano. After the Himalayan plateau it is the highest plain on Earth and Lake Titicaca, formed because several rivers drain into the plateau and have no access to the sea, is the highest navigable lake on the planet. As the environment for a major civilization it appears even less promising than the Maya lands (see page 164). There is a harsh dry season and in the wet season rains can be torrential. The lakes are very shallow and fluctuate wildly in size with seasonal floods. Temperatures vary greatly both diurnally and annually, and the high altitude and thin air exacerbate all these issues. Only a limited range of crops can be grown and yields may be very low. Straightforward traditional potato agriculture in the region yields just 2.4 tons per hectare, and even modern mechanized, petro-agriculture yields only 14.5 tons per hectare.

The ancient people of Tiwanaku developed a number of highly successful solutions to these challenges. Slopes were terraced so that they could be farmed without fields being washed away. Networks of canals irrigated areas that would otherwise be too dry. Animal husbandry developed large herds of camelids such as llamas and alpacas, with guinea pigs reared inside homes to provide extra sources of protein. But the crucial development was raised field agriculture, known as *suka kollus* by the Aymara. In areas with rich soil but that are normally susceptible to flooding, small fields are raised above the level of the plain using soil dug from canals that run between them. The water in the canals acts as a heat buffer, absorbing heat from the sun during the day and then slowly releasing it overnight to create a microclimate for the fields, protecting them from otherwise deadly frost. Edible fish are also raised in the canals and the sludge from fish droppings and decaying vegetation is dredged out and used to fertilize the fields along with camelid dung. This intensive form of agriculture allowed the Tiwanaku to grow crops that would not otherwise be viable, at yields of up to 21 tons per hectare according to modern experimental reconstructions. The fish offered an extra source of protein. Similar canal schemes were adopted for hillside terraces, with canals running along each terrace, collecting in pools and cascading down to the next terrace, irrigating the fields while controlling erosion and allowing aquaculture.

Thanks to these advances the population in the Tiwanaku region flourished. Estimates reach as high as 1.4 million, with up to 60,000 thought to have lived within the 6 square kilometres (2⅓ square miles) of central Tiwanaku and another 50,000+ in satellite settlements.

Carved human heads in the walls of the Semi-subterranean temple. As with many of the remains at Tiwanaku, it has been reconstructed and may not be accurate.
Overleaf: The entrance to the Kalasasaya temple, seen from the Semi-subterranean temple, looking towards the Ponce Monolith (also known as El Fraile, or 'The Friar').

City of Stone

The site of Tiwanaku was settled by 400 BCE, but its rise to glory really begins in around 200 CE. It became the dominant city of the Altiplano from around 500 CE until its collapse in around 1000 CE, although it probably reached its zenith around 750. During this time the Tiwanaku constructed a number of impressive stone monuments, including several huge artificial hills/pyramids. To construct these monuments they practised the most sophisticated dry-stone masonry yet discovered, of an even higher quality than that of the Inca. Large stones were shaped to fit together so perfectly that a razor blade cannot be inserted between them. Irregular stones rather than square ones were used, probably to make the masonry more earthquake proof, and in some places I-shaped copper bars were used to fasten the stones together for added protection. Many blocks were decorated with carvings, including faces and giant figures, while other monoliths and *stelae* have earned the site the nickname of 'the Stonehenge of the New World'.

The greatest structure at Tiwanaku was the Akapana, a 17-metre (55¾-feet) high terraced hill with a 61-square metre (656-square feet) base. At the summit a 15.25-square metre (164-square feet) sunken court with the marks of rectangular rooms may have hosted elite residents or been a temple. Burials of human remains, ritual objects and offerings have been found. A number of other temples are associated with the Akapana, most notably the Semi-subterranean and the Kalasasaya. The former is a sunken court with low walls studded with carved human heads. In the centre, surrounded by smaller *stelae*, is a massive *stela* known as the Bennett Monolith, after an archaeologist who did pioneering work at the site. Unfortunately, this temple bears testament to one of the main issues bedevilling archaeological research at the site, which is that it has been clumsily and probably inaccurately reconstructed, for ideological reasons (see below).

The Kalasasaya is a 130-metre (426½-feet) long platform constructed from sandstone blocks alternating with tall, upright stones, although again this may not be how it originally looked. In a sunken court on the eastern side is a massive stone statue, known as the Ponce Monolith (after another archaeologist). Exciting recent work at this temple adds weight to the Stonehenge-like identification of the site, because it seems that the Kalasasaya served as a remarkably accurate, self-correcting solar/astronomical calendar. Subsurface radar has revealed a deep shaft at the site where the observer in this monumental observatory would have stood, so more revelations could be forthcoming.

Next to the temples were buildings that may have been residences for the elite, while underneath a patio in this part of the city, archaeologists have discovered the remains of several seated individuals, facing a man with a puma-decorated sacred pottery vessel. Many of the other carvings show figures holding *keros* – ceremonial goblets that were used to serve *chicha*, or corn beer. Also in this part of the city is Tiwanaku's most famous monument, the Gateway of the Sun, which resembles a Stonehenge-like trilithon, but is actually carved from a single, enormous piece of stone that must have been hauled to the site from over 40 kilometres (24¾ miles) away. The figure carved on the gateway is known as the Staff God, and although the Inca claimed it was their progenitor god Viracocha, it is not known who he really was or what he is holding. Even this titanic monument has been moved from its original position during reconstruction work.

The common people probably lived in residences around this central complex. The picture is unclear, but some archaeologists think that neighbourhoods may have been specialized by craft or other occupation. The majority of common people probably lived in small compounds of a few single-room buildings, made from adobe bricks on stone foundations, with reed bundle roofs, surrounded by low walls. Several of these basic family unit compounds were sometimes gathered together in a 'super-compound'. Each compound was fed by a small canal and may have also been specialized for specific crafts or functions.

Empire or Ceremonial Centre?

Distinctive Tiwanaku pottery styles have been found across a broad area of the Andean region and there is little doubt that its iconography and ideology had a profound impact on the region, with elements informing cultures up to the Inca. But there is less agreement on the nature of this Tiwanaku hegemony and there is an ongoing debate about whether Tiwanaku was an empire, controlling and extracting resources from a wide area; an 'archipelago' of colonies, some set up specifically to access fertile areas or exploit local resources; a trading state with strong penetration of its commodities into its markets or a ceremonial/cultural/pilgrimage centre with no real power over other areas. There is some evidence that it was more of a loose federation of smaller states called *ayllus*, rather than a monolithic empire.

The Death and Afterlife of Tiwanaku

The youngest carbon dates from the site are from around 950 CE, although many authorities give the date of its collapse as late as 1100 CE. The reasons for its decline remain a mystery, but it is strongly suspected that a major drought may have been responsible. Even before the end, the evidence is that from around 800 CE most new building in the area involved smaller rural settlements, and that after the main city was mostly abandoned there was continued settlement in the area in small rural villages, in a return to a pre-urban lifestyle.

But the story of Tiwanaku does not end there. When the Inca came upon the site in the course of their expansion and empire-building, they quickly co-opted it for ideological purposes. Its ancient ruins, clearly predating their own origins, challenged their propaganda, which

TIWANAKU AND ATLANTIS

Perhaps inevitably, for a megalithic site with no written records, Tiwanaku has attracted many fringe theories linking it with Atlantis or an equivalent pre-historic super-civilization. One suggestion is that the complex is shaped like a port, and must once have been at sea level (before rapid continental uplift). This is linked to claims that the site actually dates back to the end of the last Ice Age. Evidence for the advanced nature of its constructors is adduced from their skill at monumental masonry and transporting huge blocks of stone, while Atlantologists point to correspondences between the story of Atlantis on the one hand, and flood myths of the Aymara and local legends of Viracocha, the culture hero from the East, on the other.

predicated their right to rule on their 'most ancient' status. To overcome this they simply claimed the site as a legendary Inca homeland, identifying the Staff God on the Gateway of the Sun as their own creator deity Viracocha, and weaving Tiwanaku into their myths.

Four hundred years after the downfall of the Incas at the hands of the conquistadors, Tiwanaku again found itself co-opted as an ideological tool. This time it was by the Bolivian government, smarting from a damaging war with its neighbour Paraguay, and seeking a national identity to rival that of the Peruvians, who had the Inca. Accordingly the government settled on Tiwanaku, commissioning a clumsy reconstruction of its monuments and carting coachloads of schoolchildren to marvel at their national icons. Even today archaeologists studying the site have to negotiate the politics surrounding it, while at the same time racing against time to preserve the ruins from uncontrolled development and exploitation that has already done considerable damage and threatens their long-term survival.

MACHU PICCHU

LOCATION: PERUVIAN ANDES

DATE OF CONSTRUCTION: 1440 CE

ABANDONED: *c* 1530 CE

BUILT BY: INCA

KEY FEATURES: CASA DEL VIGILANTE (THE GUARD HOUSE);
THE RESIDENTIAL, RELIGIOUS AND SACRED DISTRICTS; INTIHUATANA
(HITCHING-POST OF THE SUN); MAIN TEMPLE; TEMPLE OF THE THREE
WINDOWS; HOUSE OF THE WISE; PRINCESSES' BEDROOMS

In 1911 American explorer and archaeologist Hiram Bingham was led up the steep path from the Urubamba Valley, deep within the Peruvian Andes, by local guides who had promised him something special. What he found was Machu Picchu, known today as the ultimate lost city, a profoundly mysterious and affecting site that draws thousands of tourists a day despite its remote and inaccessible location. Bingham thought he had discovered Vilcabamba, final refuge of the last Inca emperor in his desperate, doomed resistance to the Spanish conquistadors, but in fact he had stumbled across something older and far stranger.

Emperor's Retreat

In Quechua, language of the Incas, Machu Picchu means 'Old Peak', a reference to the sacred peak on which it was constructed, 2,350 metres (7,709 feet) above sea level. It lies about 70 kilometres (43½ miles) northwest of the old Inca capital of Cusco and yet despite its relatively central location it was completely unknown to all but a few locals since before the Spanish conquest. Construction was probably begun by the Sapa Inca (High King) Pachacuti in around 1440 CE, or possibly his successor Yupanqui (in which case construction wouldn't have started until *c* 1460), but the site was almost certainly already abandoned by the time of the Spanish conquest in 1532.

At most around 1,000 people lived here, so lost 'city' is something of a misnomer. In fact, the geographical and economic isolation of the site, away from the major Inca highways and equipped with so little agricultural terracing that it may not even have been self-sufficient, points to the fact that Machu Picchu probably wasn't an important economic, military or administrative centre. Historians today consider that it was a personal retreat for the Inca and his family, rather like the country villa of a Roman patrician, but with spiritual and ceremonial functions at its heart, as well as a strategic role as an impregnable stronghold for the Inca elite in case of attack – a citadel rather than a city. When the Inca, his family and retinue were in attendance, the citadel was full, but at other times it was probably inhabited by only a skeleton staff of caretakers and agricultural workers to tend the terraces that surround it.

Sacred Site

Among the many mysteries of Machu Picchu is the question of why the emperor chose to build this remarkable complex in such an inaccessible and apparently unimportant spot. The solution is probably to be found in the link between landscape and spirituality that lay at the heart of Inca philosophy. The Inca revered natural features such as peaks, stones, caves and springs as *apus*, ('shrines or sacred spots'), and Machu Picchu lies in the heart of a landscape rich in spiritual significance. Both Machu Picchu itself and Huayna Picchu, the higher peak that rears up beyond it, were probably *apus*, and many of the citadel's structures are built on or from natural rock outcrops and formations, some partially sculpted or modified, which probably had spiritual significance as well. Many of the major buildings of the site have been interpreted as temples and when the Inca was in residence there was probably a whole retinue of priests and astronomers who worked with the site to determine important solar events and perform ceremonies, rituals, sacrifices and prayers.

Rough Guide to Machu Picchu

There are two main sectors of the city – the agricultural and the urban sectors. Climbing up to Machu Picchu from the southeast, the visitor first passes through the agricultural sector, which consists of more than 100 terraces, whereby the steep hillsides with their thin soils and inability to retain water are transformed into thin strips of field with stable soil, able to support

Ruined buildings at Machu Picchu. Note how the architects and builders incorporated natural outcrops of rock into their constructions.

crops. Small stone huts called *collpa* dot the terraces – these were probably storehouses.

Approaching the urban sector, the visitor passes the Casa del Vigilante – the Guard House – which commands spectacular views of the city and the Urubamba Valley. A little further along, the trail passes through the main gate and into Machu Picchu proper, which has three main districts. The Popular or Residential District is where the simplest buildings are located, and is probably where the servants and workers of the citadel lived, including the skeleton staff who maintained the place when the nobility were not in attendance. The buildings are characterized by the steep pitched roofs and include workshops and factories.

Across the Main Plaza from the Residential District, in the Sacred or Religious District, are a number of buildings that were probably temples. On a hill to one side of the plaza is one of Machu Picchu's treasures, the Intihuatana, or Hitching-Post of the Sun, a large, carved and shaped rock that culminates in a roughly square upright pillar, believed to have played a central role in Inca solar rituals and calendar calculations. Before the Spanish conquest such stones were found at the heart of all Inca communities, but the invaders destroyed all they could find in their attempt to suppress the religion. Fortunately they never discovered Machu Picchu. Other highlights of the Sacred District include the Main Temple and the deliberately roofless Temple of the Three Windows, with its characteristic trapezoid windows (believed to offer greater stability against earthquakes).

The classic view of Machu Picchu, looking over the city towards the peak of Huayna Picchu, probably taken from the Casa del Vigilante. On the right is the Residential and Industrial Zone, with its workshops and factories. In the foreground on the left is the Royal Zone, while beyond it is the Sacred or Temple Zone. In the middle is the Central Plaza. The Agricultural Zone is behind the camera.

The third district, between the Sacred District and the agricultural zone, is the Royal District, where it is believed higher status people stayed. The buildings here are of fine stonework and have evocative names such as the House of the Wise and the Princesses' Bedrooms. Rooms are trapezoid, again probably to help resist earthquake damage. Next to the Royal Palace is the Temple of the Sun, believed to have been an astronomical observatory. The Temple of the Sun has a fountain built into its very fabric, highlighting the ingenious hydrological engineering of the Incas, who used aqueducts, shaped natural channels and natural springs in the area to supply the whole citadel with running water.

Also in this district are what is believed to be the jail and the Monumental Mausoleum, where mummies were stored in niches cut into the walls and sacrifices may have been carried out. It is also believed that sacrifices or ritual torture may have been carried out in the Temple of the Condor, a partly natural rock chamber with a striking formation that resembles the outstretched wings of a condor. Grooves in the rock, possibly for channelling blood, lead down into a pit. Similar grooves are found on altars and niches elsewhere in the city. Bloodletting and sacrifice may have been a major feature of life in Machu Picchu, as evidenced by archaeological discoveries in the city of human bones bearing the marks of butchery.

Mysteries of Machu Picchu

There is no doubt that Machu Picchu exerts a powerful influence on all those who see it. Partly this is a function of the design of the city and its relations to its surroundings. Machu Picchu stands as one of the greatest monuments to Inca architecture and craftsmanship. Its layout is remarkably sympathetic to and harmonious with the natural space it occupies. Buildings appear to hang in impossible places and to have grown out of the roots of the mountain, so that the whole site works with and not against its apparently inhospitable location. Its

builders probably also designed it to reflect and pay homage to the surrounding sacred landscape in subtle ways that are hard for modern visitors to explicitly understand but that affect them nonetheless.

Another great mystery of Machu Picchu is the technical one. How could such an impressive scheme be realized in such a remote and inaccessible location, by a Bronze Age culture whose use of the wheel was restricted to children's toys? The answer is probably a combination of ingenuity, technical mastery of the arts of architecture, masonry and rock carving, and sheer manpower. In particular, the skill of the Incas is epitomized by their extraordinary dry-stone construction, in which dressed blocks of stone are fitted together without mortar, but with such precision that even the thinnest knife blade cannot be forced between them.

Perhaps the most haunting mystery of Machu Picchu is the enigma of how it came to be lost and what happened to the people who lived there. Archaeologists have unearthed about 200 skeletons of people buried on the site, but this is far fewer than the likely population of the city, suggesting that the inhabitants abandoned it or at the very least did not die off slowly enough to be buried. Plagues and epidemics are known to have wiped out whole Inca settlements, while entire communities were sometimes put to the sword as punishment or in war, but there is no evidence of any violence or destruction, or of bodies scattered around the site.

The low number of burials suggests in fact that the city was not occupied for very long, being in use for only a few decades in total. In the centre of the citadel is a large quarry, where the stone for construction came from, and it appears to have been in full use when abandoned. Perhaps after years of struggling, it was decided that it was too hard/costly to continue construction and maintenance of such a remote site, particularly if the city was the pet project of one Inca emperor or royal clan, whose enthusiasm was not shared by his/their successors.

Above all, however, the fact that knowledge of Machu Picchu was lost to all but a few locals is testament to the way in which Inca society collapsed in the face of the diseases and physical and cultural destruction the conquistadors visited upon them. A society with no formal written records (the Incas had no writing) relied on oral transmission and a continuity of scholarship for its cultural transmission and such education was restricted to a small elite. The impact of the Spanish conquest was too much for such a fragile system and it was all too easy for a remote city, far off the main highways along a difficult trail that would have been overrun by jungle within a year without maintenance, to fall off the map. But the Incas' tragedy is our blessing, for it means the lost city survived the ravages of the Spanish conquest.

The Future of Machu Picchu

Ironically, however, for a site whose reputation rests on having survived untouched for more than five centuries, there are now serious concerns about the future of Machu Picchu. The pressures of mass tourism are threatening the fabric of the site and the surrounding ecology. It is a World Heritage Site but is officially 'at risk' and Peru has been warned that the site might be stripped of its 'Heritage' status if Peru does not take steps to preserve it. The enduring mysteries of Machu Picchu may never be solved, but tragically they may outlast the site itself.

A view through a doorway framing Huayna Picchu (Quechua for 'Young Peak'). This was a sacred peak to the Inca, who constructed a trail to its summit, upon which they built more temples and terraces. To alleviate the pressure of huge numbers of tourists, only 400 visitors a day are permitted to make the difficult climb up to the peak.

RECOMMENDED READING

Atkinson, Austen, *Lost Civilizations: Rediscovering Ancient Sites Through New Technologies* (Watson-Guptill Publications, 2003)

Bahn, Paul (Ed), *Lost Cities: 50 Discoveries in World Archaeology* (Phoenix Illustrated, 1999)

Baudez, Claude and Picasso, Sydney, *Lost Cities of the Maya* (New Horizons, 1992)

Blegen, Carl William, *Troy and the Trojans* (Thames and Hudson, 1963)

Butterworth, Alex and Laurence, Ray, *Pompeii: The Living City* (Phoenix, 2006)

Cottrell, Leonard, *Lost Cities* (Robert Hale Ltd, 1957)

Curtis, J.E. and Tallis, Nigel (Eds), *Forgotten Empire: The World of Ancient Persia* (British Museum Press, 2005)

Diamond, Jared, *Collapse: How Societies Choose to Fail or Survive* (Allen Lane, 2005)

Dobbins, J.J. and Foss, P.W. (Eds), *The World of Pompeii* (Routledge, 2007)

Doumas, Christos, *Thera: Pompeii of the Ancient Aegean* (Thames and Hudson, 1983)

Fagan, Brian (Ed), *Discovery! Unearthing the New Treasures of Archaeology* (Thames and Hudson, 2007)

Guaitoli, Maria Teresa and Rambaldi, Simone, *Lost Cities From the Ancient World* (White Star, 2006)

Harrison, Peter D., *The Lords of Tikal: Rulers of an Ancient Maya City* (Thames and Hudson, 2000)

Jacques, Claude and Freeman, Michael, *Angkor: Cities and Temples* (Thames and Hudson, 1997)

Kenoyer, Jonathan Mark, *Ancient Cities of the Indus Valley Civilization* (Oxford University Press, 1998)

Lane Fox, Robin, *The Classical World: An Epic History from Homer to Hadrian* (Allen Lane, 2005)

Leick, Gwendolyn, *Mesopotamia: The Invention of the City* (Penguin, 2002)

Levy, Joel, *Lost Histories* (Vision, 2006)

Levy, Joel, *The Atlas of Atlantis and Other Lost Civilisations* (Godsfield Press, 2007)

Macdonald, Colin F., *Knossos* (Folio Society, 2005)

Maqsood, Rosalyn, *Petra: A Traveller's Guide* (Garnet Publishing, 1996)

Owens, E.J., *The City in the Greek and Roman World* (Routledge, 1992)

Stefoff, Rebecca, *Finding the Lost Cities: The Golden Age of Archaeology* (British Museum Press, 1997)

Tomlinson, R.A., *From Mycenae to Constantinople: Evolution of the Ancient City* (Routledge, 1992)

Various, *Mysteries of the Ancient Ones*, a special edition of *Scientific American* (2005)

RECOMMENDED WEBSITES

Generally useful for ancient cities and history

Archaeology magazine: www.archaeology.org

BBC Ancient History: www.bbc.co.uk/history/ancient/

Catholic Encyclopaedia:
    www.newadvent.org/cathen/index.html

Common-place: The Interactive Journal of Early
    American Life: www.common-place.org

Current Archaeology magazine:
    www.archaeology.co.uk

Digital Egypt for Universities:
    www.digitalegypt.ucl.ac.uk

Egyptology Online: www.egyptologyonline.com

Encyclopaedia Romana:
    http://penelope.uchicago.edu/~grout/
    encyclopaedia_romana/index.html

Foundation of the Hellenic World:
    www.fhw.gr/index_en.html

Jewish Encylopedia:
    www.jewishencyclopedia.com/index.jsp

Livius: Articles on Ancient History: www.livius.org

LookLex: http://i-cias.com

LookLex Enyclopaedia:
    http://lexicorient.com/e.o/index.htm

Metropolitan Museum of Art: www.metmuseum.org

Minnesota State University Latin American Prehistory:
    www.mnsu.edu/emuseum/prehistory/latinamerica/

National Geographic News:
    http://news.nationalgeographic.com/news/index.html

Natural History magazine: http://nhmag.com/

Prehistoric Archaeology of the Aegean:
    http://projectsx.dartmouth.edu/history/bronze_age/

Smithsonian magazine: www.smithsonianmag.com

Tour Egypt Feature Stories:
    www.touregypt.net/featurestories/

Websites dealing with specific sites

CAHOKIA

The Mississippian Moundbuilders and Their Artefacts:
    www.mississippian-artifacts.com

Cahokia Mounds State Historic Site:
    www.cahokiamounds.com

CHICHEN ITZA

American Egypt: www.americanegypt.com

ENTREMONT

The Gauls in Provence: The Oppidum of Entremont:
    www.culture.gouv.fr/culture/arcnat/entremont/en/

FUJIWARA-KYO

Asuka Historical Museum:
    www.asukanet.gr.jp/asukahome/

HARAPPA

The Ancient Indus Valley: www.harappa.com

KNOSSOS

The British School at Athens: www.bsa.ac.uk/knosos/

MOHENJO-DARO

Mohenjo-daro, the Ancient Indus Valley City:
    www.mohenjodaro.net

TIWANAKU

Penn Museum Research Project:
    www.museum.upenn.edu/new/research/
    Exp_Rese_Disc/Americas/tiwanaku/index.shtml

INDEX

ACKNOWLEDGMENTS

The author and publishers would like to extend their grateful thanks to the following for reading sections of the book and for offering their expert advice and guidance on the history of particular sites: Gina Barnes, John J. Dobbins, Aidan Dodson, Damian Evans, Shahina Farid, Andrew George, Bill Iseminger, C.T. Keally, Jonathan Mark Kenoyer, Andreas Kropp, Matthew W. Stolper and Ken Wardle. Any errors that remain are entirely the responsibility of the author. The author would also like to thank Kate Parker.

Thanks to the following for allowing their images to be used in this book, and especially to Andrew George and Martin Schøyen for the drawing on page 31:

Front cover: ©Neil Emmerson/Robert Harding; back cover (left to right): ©iStockphoto.com/Marisa Allegra Williams, ©iStockphoto.com/Salem, ©iStockphoto.com/John Said;
page 1: ©iStockphoto.com/Salem; page 2: ©Pictures Colour Library; page 3: ©iStockphoto.com/John Said; page 4–5: ©Pictures Colour Library; page 6 (main image): ©iStockphoto.com/Amanda Lewis; page 7: ©Pictures Colour Library; page 9: ©Pictures Colour Library; page 15: ©Pictures Colour Library; pages 16–21: ©The Çatalhöyük Research Project/Jason Quinlan; page 23: ©iStockphoto.com/Jakub Sobczak; page 24: ©Robert Harding; page 27: ©iStockphoto.com/Asli Orter; page 29: ©Nico Tondini/Robert Harding; page 31: ©Andrew George; page 32: ©iStockphoto.com/John Said; page 35: ©Pictures Colour Library; page 37: ©iStockphoto.com/Dean Robertson; page 38: ©iStockphoto.com/Adrian Beesley; page 41: ©iStockphoto.com/Adrian Beesley; page 43: ©Pictures Colour Library; page 44: ©iStockphoto.com/Adrian Beesley; page 47: ©Pictures Colour Library; page 49: ©iStockphoto.com/Richard Cano; pages 50–51: ©Michael Jenner/Robert Harding; page 53: ©iStockphoto.com/Adrian Beesley; pages 54–55: ©Pictures Colour Library; page 56: ©iStockphoto.com/Karen Moller; page 57: ©iStockphoto.com/Heather Faye Bath; page 59: ©iStockphoto.com/domin23; pages 60–61: ©Christopher Rennie/Robert Harding; page 62: ©Pictures Colour Library; page 65: ©Cubo Images/Robert Harding; page 67: ©CGavin Hellier/Robert Harding; pages 68–69: ©Marco Simoni/Robert Harding; page 73: ©iStockphoto.com/Marisa Allegra Williams; pages 74–75: ©Tony Waltham/Robert Harding: page 76: ©iStockphoto.com/Danilo Ascione; page 77: ©iStockphoto.com/DHuss; page 78: ©iStockphoto.com/Danilo Ascione; page 81: ©iStockphoto.com/Paul Cowan; page 82–83: ©Pictures Colour Library; page 85: ©iStockphoto.com/Paul Cowan; pages 87–91: ©Troels Myrup Kristensen; page 93: ©Sergio Pitamitz/Robert Harding; pages 96–97: ©Pictures Colour Library; page 98: ©iStockphoto.com/Robert Kerton; page 101: ©Reza, Webistan/CORBIS; pages 102–103: ©Pictures Colour Library; page 107: ©Andrew McConnell/Robert Harding; pages 108–109: ©JJ Travel/Robert Harding; page 113: courtesy of Alan Marshall; pages 114–115: ©Pictures Colour Library; page 116: ©iStockphoto.com/Karen Moller; page 119: ©iStockphoto.com/Amanda Lewis; pages 120–121: ©Pictures Colour Library; page 123: ©iStockphoto.com/Amanda Lewis; page 125: ©Pictures Colour Library; page 127 ©Robert Harding; pages 132–133: ©Luca Tettoni/Robert Harding; page 134: ©Robert Harding; page 137: ©iStockphoto.com/Simon Gurney; pages 138–139: ©Pictures Colour Library; page 145: ©The Yomiuri Shimbun; page 147: ©Rob Cousins/Robert Harding; page 148: ©Cahokia Mounds State Historic Site; page 149: ©Richard A. Cooke/Corbis; page 152-153: ©Michael S. Lewis/Corbis; page 155: ©iStockphoto.com/Daniel Fiverson; page 156: ©iStockphoto.com/Daniel Fiverson; page 158: ©Walter Rawlings/Robert Harding; page 159: courtesy of Alan Marshall; page 161: ©Charles & Josette Lenars/Corbis; page 165: ©iStockphoto.com/Valerie Loiseleux; pages 166–167: ©Pictures Colour Library; page 169: ©iStockphoto.com/Luis Seco; page 171: ©Sybil Sassoon/Robert Harding; page 172: ©iStockphoto.com/Brian Raisbeck; page 175: ©iStockphoto.com/Tatiana Murcova; pages 176–177: ©Christophe Boisvieux/Corbis; page 181: ©Pictures Colour Library; pages 182–183: ©Christopher Rennie/Robert Harding; page 185: ©iStockphoto.com/Maxime Vige